Praise for Brilliant Psychology

'A really enjoyable read and an excellent introduction to psychology. *Brilliant Psychology* is packed with examples and insights that bring the subject alive.'

Professor Kate Jeffery, behavioural neuroscientist

'If you want a better understanding of psychology and what it can tell you about yourself and others, this concise and readable summary will do the job. It presents key psychological findings and insights in a lively, accessible and informative way. A great starting point for the novice, and overview for the more experienced.'

Dr Lucy Johnstone, consultant clinical psychologist

'This is a chocolate box of a book that manages to combine psychological theory, real life experiences, practical tasks and human insights in an accessible and enjoyable way. It covers a vast expanse of psychology including learning, memory, child development, happiness and psychological problems and should be read by anyone who wants to understand both why they and those around them think and behave the way they do.'

Jane Ogden, Professor of Health Psychology, University of Surrey

brilliant

psychology

brilliant

psychology

How to understand yourself and other people

Louise Deacon

PEARSON

Harlow, England • London • New York • Boston • San Francisco • Toronto • Sydney • Auckland • Singapore • Hong Kong
Tokyo • Seoul • Taipei • New Delhi • Cape Town • São Paulo • Mexico City • Madrid • Amsterdam • Munich • Paris • Milan

PEARSON EDUCATION

Edinburgh Gate
Harlow CM20 2JE
United Kingdom
Tel: +44 (0)1279 623623
Website: www.pearson.co

First published 2013 (prir

© Pearson Education Lim

The right of Louise Deacon to be identified as author of this work has been asserted by her in accordance with the Copyright, Designs and Patents Act 1988.

Pearson Education is not responsible for the content of third-party internet sites.

ISBN: 978-0-273-77946-9 (print)
    978-0-273-78040-3 (PDF)
    978-0-273-78039-7 (ePub)

British Library Cataloguing-in-Publication Data
A catalogue record for the print edition is available from the British Library

Library of Congress Cataloging-in-Publication Data
A catalog record for the print edition is available from the Library of Congress

10 9 8 7 6 5 4 3
16 15

Illustrations by Bill Piggins
Print edition typeset in 10/14pt Plantin Std by 30
Printed in Great Britain by Henry Ling Limited, at the Dorset Press, Dorchester, DT1 1HD

NOTE THAT ANY PAGE CROSS-REFERENCES REFER TO THE PRINT EDITION

Contents

About the author

Louise Deacon is a clinical psychologist in the NHS with 20 years' experience of using psychology to help adults solve their personal problems. Her current post is at Kingston Hospital and she is also Senior Tutor at the University of Surrey on the Clinical Psychology training programme.

Introduction

One of the most powerful forces in the world lies in between your ears. The human mind, working in combination with other minds, can achieve almost anything: dismantle the atom, build a cathedral, fly to the moon.

And you are already a psychologist. You already have a good ability to understand, influence and predict the minds of others – you do it every day. Your ability to understand people is highly significant – some psychologists believe that your ability to understand other minds is probably *why you have a mind at all*.

Think back to the conversations you have had or heard in the last couple of days. How much of the discussion was about friends, relatives, workmates, the boss or people you know from the media – actors, royalty, TV personalities?

This fascination with other people is one of the keys to our human nature: this text reveals why. Yet we take this interest in people for granted; it seems so familiar and natural that we don't even think about it.

That is why we need psychology.

Our own common-sense understanding of people can only take us so far; it cannot answer some of the most basic questions about our human experiences. For example, why do we fall in love? What makes us intelligent? Our intuitive psychology often fails to explain our individual differences, for example, why do some people get nervous about public speaking while others do not? Why do some people struggle to show affection and others seem too 'needy'?

As well as these everyday psychological puzzles, the extremes of human behaviour often completely defy common sense. We hear about atrocities on the news and wonder – what drives people to behave like this?

To discover the answers, we need to take a deeper look at ourselves.

Psychologists have been doing this for the past 130 years and this text contains some of their key insights. The material in this text will give you a better understanding of yourself and other people, and is practical, showing how you can apply psychology in your own life.

What is psychology?

Psychology is the attempt to transform our everyday understanding of the mind into a scientific one. The first psychology lab was founded by Wilhelm Wundt in Leipzig in 1879. William James, the founder of psychology in America, defined it in 1890 as 'the science of mental life'.

But our mental experiences are difficult to study – they are subjective and from the inside, seem miraculous. We all have a vivid stream of consciousness: a constantly shifting mindscape of thoughts, impulses, moods, memories, feelings and daydreams. With our words we can create experiences in other minds: images, ideas, anger, happiness, hope, despair. And this is only the part of the mind we have access to. Our conscious awareness is just a glimpse of its workings.

Wilhelm Wundt tried to analyse the contents of people's consciousness by asking them to describe their experiences.

But William James did not believe we can study ourselves by describing the contents of our minds like this, and said it was like 'turning up the gas quickly to see how the darkness works'.

When psychology lost its mind

So in 1913 psychologist John Watson declared that conscious experience could not be studied scientifically at all. He decided there was no point in speculating about what goes on in the mind – it was all too subjective. He believed that rather than trying to peer inside our heads, we should instead understand ourselves by studying the links between our behaviour and the environment. For 50 years, psychology tended to only deal with observable facts, a branch of psychology known as behaviourism.

During the behaviourism era we furthered our scientific understanding of ourselves by concentrating on what people actually did, however our mental processes remained a puzzle.

Today, advances in science and technology have given us new ways of studying and understanding ourselves. For example, with brain-imaging techniques we can almost literally look inside our heads and see which parts of the brain light up when we think or feel.

Psychology has again become the science of mental life as well as behaviour, and has finally begun to reveal some of the mysteries of the mind.

Publisher's acknowledgements

The publishers are grateful to Sonja Lyubomirsky for permission to reproduce the figure on p.246 from *The How of Happiness*, Piatkus, 2010.

Acknowledgement is also made to the IPIP and Lewis Goldberg for use of the adapted mini personality questionnaires from the International Personality Item Pool at www.ipip.ori.org (*A Scientific Collaboratory for the Development of Advanced Measures of Personality Traits and Other Individual Differences*). Public domain internet website.

CHAPTER 1

Understanding your intelligent mind

You have an intelligent mind: you have a curiosity which made you pick up this book and you can understand these words. But what is your mind and how does it work? And what makes you an intelligent, conscious being?

What your mind is for

Psychologist Steven Pinker says that although the mind seems miraculous we do not need to use any mystical concepts to explain it. The mind is just the activity of the brain, and the brain is like any other biological organ such as the heart, liver or lungs. The brain evolved because it plays an important role in keeping us alive. Relative to our body weight, the human brain is bigger than in other animals, but we are just one of many species who have a complex nervous system. As Steven Pinker puts it, 'the human brain is a swollen and warped version of the brains of other mammals'.

The brain evolved because it directs our behaviour in ways that increase the likelihood of our survival. Our minds help us solve the practical problems of living, such as finding food and shelter.

We are a social animal, and one of the problems of living is getting on with other people. We face problems such as enlisting other people's cooperation and spotting when someone is trying

our minds are for dealing
with other minds

to take advantage of us. Figuring out how to deal with other people is a complex task: so our minds are also for dealing with other minds.

We solve the practical and social problems of living by changing our behaviour and adopting new strategies. In other words, our brains give us the ability to learn from our experience. Our capacity for learning is vastly greater than that of the other animals and is one of the distinguishing features of the human mind.

How do we learn?

During the behaviourist years, psychologists concentrated on understanding how we learn. They studied the links between the stimuli in the environment and our behavioural response. They discovered that some of our learning can be accounted for by two basic conditioning processes: classical and operant conditioning. These conditioning processes can take place outside our control, against our will and sometimes without our knowledge.

1 Classical conditioning

Classical conditioning is where a trigger in the environment sets off an automatic bodily or emotional response because of a learned association. An example is that many of us hate the way hospitals smell. Because we have been in hospitals and felt anxious, the smell of the hospital produces a feeling of unease. Other examples are the sound of the dentist's drill triggering fear, or walking into the kitchen and feeling hunger. Classical conditioning can explain many of our everyday automatic reactions.

This type of learning was discovered in 1903 by Ivan Pavlov, a Russian physiologist who was studying digestion in dogs. He noticed that the dogs started salivating as soon as they heard the clicking sound of the machine that delivered their food. The dogs had formed an association between the clicking noise and food.

In 1920, John Watson and Rosalie Rayner carried out a famous, if unethical, study of classical conditioning with 'Little Albert', a ten-month-old baby. Watson conditioned Albert to be scared of a white rat, by making a loud noise with a gong every time the baby saw the rat. After seven pairings, Albert cried when he saw the rat, and was also scared of other white, furry things, such as a Santa Claus beard.

Profile: John Broadus Watson

John Watson (1878-1958) came from a poor and troubled family in rural America, his alcoholic father abandoning his mother when Watson was aged 13. Watson had to work hard to get his education, supporting himself by earning money as a waiter and a janitor. When he carried out the 'Little Albert' experiment with Rosalie Rayner, a graduate student, he was an internationally renowned psychologist at Johns Hopkins University and at the height of his career. He was also married with two children, but it soon came to light that he and Rosalie Rayner were having an affair. This was considered scandalous at the time; he was forced to resign and no other university would offer him a post.

Instead, he moved to New York, worked in advertising and became a millionaire. He married Rosalie Rayner and they had two children. Rosalie died at the age of 36, and it is thought that Watson never fully recovered from her loss.

Watson wrote books about his theories of childrearing, influential at the time, arguing that children should be given very little affection. He is the maternal grandfather of the American actress Mariette Hartley, who has written about her grandfather's legacy of distant, emotionless childrearing. She believes it caused psychological damage to herself and her mother, leading to their struggles with emotional intimacy and alcohol abuse. In later life, Watson admitted he had not known enough about childrearing and was said to have regretted writing about it.

▶

Not long before his death, Watson's achievements were finally recognised by the American Psychological Association and he was given an award for his contributions to psychology.

Classical conditioning can explain how we develop phobias. It may also account for some sexual fetishes. In 1966 Rachman showed pictures of a pair of black boots with pictures of a naked woman to a group of men. After repeated pairings of these pictures, the men became aroused after seeing the picture of the boots alone.

This type of conditioning may also explain why some advertisements work. Advertisers repeatedly pair their brand with stimuli that will produce an automatic positive reaction, in the hope that we will automatically associate their product with that positive feeling. For example, soft drinks manufacturers sponsoring the Olympic Games hope the feelings of pride and excitement connected with the Games will become associated with their brand. This automatic positive response may be enough to tip the balance so you reach for their product on the supermarket shelf.

brilliant insight

We can be classically conditioned and know nothing about it. If you drink alcohol regularly, have you ever noticed that it affects you some times more than others? Or that one drink has a bigger effect on you than another, even though they contain the same amount of alcohol? When you drink something alcoholic, your body reacts by compensating and counteracting the effects of the drug on your body.

When you are in the habit of having the same drink in the same place, your body will begin the compensatory response automatically, because of classical conditioning. The cues such as opening the bottle of wine and settling on the couch will trigger your body to start counteracting the alcohol.

But if you have an unfamiliar drink, for example, beer when you are used to drinking wine, or you are in an unfamiliar place such as on holiday, your body does not associate these situations with alcohol. It does not automatically start to compensate, and so you will feel more intoxicated.

Classical conditioning also explains the mystery of drug-related deaths. Drug deaths are always called 'overdoses', but often the victims have taken no more of the drug than usual. But they were in an unfamiliar place, doing something differently, even in a different room when they took the fatal dose. Psychologist Shepard Siegel describes a case of a patient who was taking morphine for a medical condition. The patient normally took the morphine in his bedroom, a dimly lit room. One day he took the medicine in his more brightly lit living room, and even though it was his normal dose, it killed him.

2 Operant conditioning

Our learning is obviously not restricted to our automatic reflexes and emotions – we are capable of complex behaviours, such as baking a cake or driving to work. Building on the work of the earlier psychologist Edward Thorndike, B. F. Skinner studied the type of learning that in 1938 he called 'operant conditioning'. Operant conditioning is where we learn because of the consequences of our actions. We are more or less likely to repeat a behaviour, depending on the kind of consequences. The consequences are of three types:

- Positive reinforcement: rewarding, enjoyable, pleasant consequences, such as affection, compliments, money or food. We are likely to repeat positively reinforced behaviour. So when we get praised by our boss for our hard work we are likely to do more of the same.

- Negative reinforcement: the removal of an unpleasant stimulus. For example, we wash to remove dirt or smell and we clean up to get rid of mess or to stop our partner's nagging. Other examples are taking a headache pill and studying to avoid failing an exam. We are likely to repeat behaviour that is negatively reinforced.

● Punishment: an unpleasant consequence that reduces the likelihood of our behaviour being repeated – a telling-off, a parking fine, a driving ban, prison.

Skinner believed all our behaviour is determined by positive and negative reinforcement and punishment. For example, gambling is reinforced by winning, and the unpredictable nature of this reinforcement makes it particularly powerful. Winning only happens from time to time at random intervals – this is known as a 'variable schedule' of reinforcement. A variable schedule of reinforcement makes us persist with the gambling behaviour because we have learned that a reward will come in time if we carry on.

brilliant insight

Skinner's work made people realise that punishment alone is often an ineffective way of shaping people's behaviour, because it does not teach people what to do, only what not to do. The main thing we learn from being punished is how to avoid further punishment. This often involves engaging in other types of undesirable behaviour. For example, your local council decides it wants people to cut down on waste, so it charges them for putting out extra bags of rubbish. But far from cutting down on waste, people start dumping their rubbish in the countryside instead.

These principles of reinforcement, although simple, have led to effective methods of behaviour change, widely used in workplaces, schools and prisons. Techniques for managing everyday behaviour problems in children, such as those shown on TV programmes such as 'Supernanny', are based on these principles.

Is there something you would like to change? Try thinking like a behaviourist: identify the reinforcements that are maintaining the behaviour, and if it is appropriate to do so, change the reinforcements to encourage different behaviour.

brilliant example

Behaviour problem: Every time you pass the sweet shop on the way to school, your young child demands sweets and if you say no she cries and sits on the ground, refusing to budge. For a quiet life you sometimes give in, but now every day going to school is a battle.

Analysis: You and your child are reinforcing each other in this behaviour. The demanding, crying and refusal to move is maintained by a variable schedule of positive reinforcement when you buy her sweets. She is negatively reinforcing your behaviour: when you buy the sweets she stops crying.

Solution: Create positive reinforcements for the behaviour you want. Set up a reward system, such as a star chart so she gets a sticker and praise for 'walking quietly straight past the shop to school'. Or she could get sweets as a reward when you arrive at school. Once a behaviour has been established, the rewards can be faded out over time.

Behaviourism reached a peak in Skinner's famous book, *Beyond Freedom and Dignity*. He believed that everything we do is determined by our environment, therefore there is no such thing as free will or choice. So we can't take personal credit – or responsibility – for our actions. Skinner argued that society would be much happier if we accepted this, and organised our lives according to behavioural principles.

The behaviourists dreamed that one day we would understand ourselves without any need to look inside our minds. But not everybody shared this vision. Many thinkers continued to study subjective human experience. For example, the Gestalt psychologists, led by Max Wertheimer, focused on visual perception, our experience of seeing things in the world. The humanistic psychologists, such as Carl Rogers and Abraham Maslow, were interested in even broader aspects of human experience such as creativity, emotional needs, love and happiness.

Sigmund Freud went even further and wanted to understand not only our conscious experiences, but our unconscious experiences, too. He believed that the largest part of our mental life is governed by unconscious processes: by motivations, emotions and impulses operating underneath our awareness.

The failure of behaviourism

By about the middle of the twentieth century or so, it became obvious to many that conditioning fails to explain all our behaviour.

For example, rewards don't always reinforce behaviours in humans. Psychologists Lepper and Greene gave children puzzles to work on. Some were rewarded for doing so, some were not. When they gave the puzzles to the children at a later date, they discovered that the rewarded children were far less likely to play with the puzzles again of their own accord. The children reasoned that because they had been rewarded before, the puzzles could not have been satisfying in themselves. The reward had reduced their intrinsic motivation.

And we do not need to experience consequences in order to learn. Albert Bandura pointed out that we can learn from watching others. In one of his most famous studies, he showed how children learn from adults. In this study, a group of children watched an adult playing with a Bobo doll, a large inflatable toy with a weight at the base so it springs upright when pushed or hit. Some of the children watched an adult playing aggressively with the doll, punching it and kicking it. The children, especially the boys, who saw the adult playing aggressively, were more likely to punch, hit and throw the doll themselves. And the behaviour was not just a copy of the adults; they came up with new ways to hit the doll.

Bandura concluded that humans do not just respond to rewards or punishments, but are active, motivated agents. To understand learning we cannot merely look at behaviours, we also need to look at processes inside the mind such as perception, thinking, memory, attention and decision-making. These processes are called 'cognition'.

A revolutionary way of understanding the mind

Psychologists, inspired by the invention of computers, realised there was a new way to understand the mind. They realised our brains could be seen as an 'information-processing' device. In the 1950s Herbert Simon showed that psychological processes could be simulated with a computer.

In psychology this view of the mind as an 'information-processing machine' is known as the cognitive revolution. Ulric Neisser coined the term for this new approach in the title of his 1967 book, *Cognitive Psychology*.

How the brain works

The brain is made of bundles of cells called neurons, which can fire a tiny electrical impulse. So a brain cell is like a switch that can be on or off. Anything that switches on and off can be used to transmit information. For example, you can send a message to someone by switching your torch on and off, if you know Morse code.

Like using different patterns of switching your torch on and off with Morse code to convey information, the brain uses patterns of neurons switching on and off. This is the same basic way a computer works. A computer conveys information using tiny electronic switches.

So in your mind, information is conveyed and manipulated by brain cells passing electrical impulses to each other in complex ways according to a complicated code. Everything from recognising your partner's face to understanding the concept of justice is achieved by patterns of neurons firing.

brilliant insight

The patterns of neurons firing in your brain right at this moment have just enabled you to understand the concept of patterns of neurons firing.

Sensory perception

Information from the outside world and inside your body comes via your five senses. Sensory receptor cells, such as the cells of the eye's retina, detect physical changes and relay this information to the brain using electrical impulses. Our minds process this information using further complex patterns of electrical impulses between cells.

All this information processing takes considerable effort: your brain makes up 2 per cent of your body weight, yet uses 20 per cent of your energy.

Donald Hebb discovered that when we learn, our brain structure is changed. When the same brain pathways are used repeatedly, neurons form new connections with each other. The phrase 'neurons which fire together, wire together' is known as Hebb's law.

when we learn our brain structure is changed

The human imagination

But what makes the mind so powerful is that we are not limited to processing information about 'reality'. We can combine the information in our heads to come up with new ideas or concepts. We can conjure up in our minds something that doesn't exist. We can imagine things that are physically impossible, such as suddenly growing wings and flying off to live happily on Mars. The power of our minds is that we, in the words of Lewis Carroll, can imagine 'six impossible things before breakfast'.

So we are capable of immense creativity and invention.

Language

The human mind is even more potent because we can share information with other people via language. When we combine our thinking and imagination with others and build on the insights and technology of the previous generation we become a formidable force.

In language, our minds transform the patterns of neurons firing into a different kind of code: the sounds we make with our mouth. Spoken language is just a code whereby we agree that certain noises stand for something else. So the sound 'apple' stands for an apple.

All human societies have language. The linguist and thinker Noam Chomsky argues that our ability for language is hardwired into our brains. He believes that although languages vary, they all have the same underlying basic form, a 'universal grammar' – for example, all languages have nouns and verbs.

Does language have to be learned from others? The surprising answer is – no.

Steven Pinker points out in his book *The Language Instinct* that when groups of people are deprived of language they spontaneously generate their own. For example, groups of deaf children who have not had the opportunity to learn an existing sign language will invent a new one. Signing was invented by deaf people, not hearing people as many assume, and sign languages are almost as complex as spoken ones. However, language is something we only generate with others. If a deaf child only interacts with hearing people, she will not develop a sign language of her own.

Memory

The above processes could not work without an information storage system. Memory can be classified into different types, but the most basic distinction is between short-term memory, also known as working memory, and long-term memory.

Working memory

Psychologist Alan Baddely sees working memory as a mental 'blackboard' or work space, closely akin to our sense of consciousness. Working memory is not just a store, but it has a role in active thinking and accesses the information most relevant to the problem at that moment. Our working memory can access information from the long-term memory.

exercise   What is your working memory span?

Read through the list below once. Try to keep the words in mind then look away and write them down in order.

Fake   Jumper   Axe   Book   Apple   Tin   Rope   Smile   Ale
Hope   Call   Sheet

Most adults can keep between five and ten items in short-term memory; the average is seven. In a well-known paper from 1956, titled 'The magical number seven, plus or minus two', George Miller observed that on average, we can only hold seven chunks of information at a time in our short-term memories. A chunk of information is anything that is a meaningful whole – this could be a single item such as one digit, or a bigger number. For example, the date 9/11 is a meaningful whole for most people now.

Long-term memory

Information in your short-term memory may be transferred into your long-term memory, but we do not have the capacity or need to store absolutely all of it. So the way verbal memory works is that you do not store all the actual words. Your memory encodes the underlying meaning, just the gist of what you hear.

brilliant insight

During an argument with someone, have you ever heard yourself saying 'I never said that! All I said was...' You try to put them right, but they insist you said something completely different. This is because they misunderstood your meaning at the time. But this is all they will be able to remember, they will not be able to recall your exact words. The gist or sense is the only thing to stay in long-term memory, not the words themselves.

Memories are stored into 'schemas', organised bodies of knowledge in our minds. These schemas actively affect the way we remember information. If information does not seem to make sense in terms of our existing schemas, our brains will change it to fit. This was discovered by Frederick Bartlett in a well-known study in 1932. He asked people to remember an American Indian folk tale called 'The War of the Ghosts', which did not make sense to Western ears, with odd supernatural happenings. In the story, one of the characters dies and 'something black came out of his mouth'. People remembered this as 'he foamed at the mouth'. The information had been adjusted so it made more sense in terms of existing schemas.

Our minds also take information we have learned later, then weave it into our memories. In another classic study in 1974, Elisabeth Loftus and John Palmer showed people a film clip of a traffic accident, then asked them one of two questions:

How fast was the car going when it *hit* the other car?

or

How fast was the car going when it *smashed into* the other car?

The people asked about the car that had 'smashed' into the other, estimated that the cars were going faster than those asked about the car that had 'hit' the other.

A week later, Loftus and Palmer asked them another question about the film clip: 'Did you see any broken glass?' The ones who heard the word 'smashed' were far more likely to say yes. In fact, there was no broken glass in the clip. The word 'smashed' had evoked ideas that became incorporated into people's memories.

False memories

Is our long-term memory so active and creative that it reaches a point that we can 'remember' things that are not real?

Elizabeth Loftus and Jacqueline Pickrell wanted to discover if it was possible to implant false memories into people. They told a group of subjects that they had been lost in a shopping mall when they were children, claiming they had spoken to their families who had told them about the incident. When they asked people to recall details of the incident, about a quarter of them said they could remember it, and they even supplied extra details about what happened – even though the story was made up.

Our ability to recall things that are not real is a serious problem for the reliability of eyewitness testimonies in court, and there's more in Chapter 8 on the devastating consequences this can have for people's lives. Loftus carried out her work to throw light on the 'recovered memory' debate, and she showed it is possible for false memories of childhood abuse to be unwittingly implanted by misguided therapists. Loftus' work has earned her many awards, but also harassment and even death threats from people on the other side of the debate.

🢅 brilliant impact

How to improve your memory

Research shows that learning information in short sessions, with 24 hours in between, is better than one long session. But thinking deeply about your material is the best way to help you remember it. Putting in active effort will help you encode, store and retrieve the information.

Memory works in these three stages – encoding, storage and retrieval – and can fail at each stage. Either the information does not go into your mind, or it does not stay there, or you cannot find it. This last type of memory failure is the 'tip of the tongue' phenomena, when you know you know something, but cannot recall it.

Methods of processing information deeply include:

- Organise: Sort your information into a structure, for example, categories or a hierarchy that shows how the information links together. When your material is linked together, remembering one part should trigger the memory of another.

- Teach: Conveying your material to someone else will improve your understanding and so it will be easier to recall.

- Elaborate: Think about what your material means, what questions it raises and what it implies for other aspects of the issue.

- Summarise: Pull out the main conceptual points.

- Relate: Try to relate the new information to what you already know to make links with your existing knowledge, which will become a cue for the new knowledge.

- Transform: Turn the material into a different type of information, such as pictures or diagrams.

Two ways of thinking?

The information we have in our memory is manipulated by our thinking processes. Psychologist Daniel Kahneman says we have two systems for thinking. First, there is the unconscious system: all the impressions, decisions and understandings that take place in your mind effortlessly and automatically he calls system 1. This type of thinking is fast and is not under our control. For example, when you see a cake, you instinctively recognise it as a cake, you anticipate its delicious taste and have the automatic urge to reach for a slice.

Second, there is a conscious, deliberate system for thinking. This type of thinking is slower, takes effort and is under our control. Kahneman calls it system 2, and this is the type of thinking we equate with our 'conscious, reasoning selves'. So, as your fingers begin to twitch towards the cake knife, your system 2 kicks in. You tell yourself that eating the cake does not fit into your weight loss plan. You look at the thick layer of icing and do mental calculations of the calories you have already eaten today. Your system 2 deliberates over whether to go ahead with the plans of system 1.

our minds are like a troubled coalition government

So our minds are like a troubled coalition government, as system 1 and system 2 battle it out. And which part of our minds is more in charge? Is it the automatic, unconscious system, or our conscious, reasoning selves? Read Chapter 8 to find out about some research that reveals a surprising answer.

Was Freud right?

Although many of Sigmund Freud's more colourful ideas, like the concept of 'penis envy', have not stood the test of time, most psychologists believe he was right in his basic view that much of our behaviour is influenced by unconscious processes. It is now generally accepted that we can have emotions without conscious awareness of them, and our minds can perceive things without us knowing it. We are only aware of a small proportion of the activity in our minds.

The limitations of the information-processing approach

Studying cognitive processes has led to major advances in psychology, taking it far beyond the restricted view of behaviourism. We now understand how our ability to think, remember, imagine and use language has taken us to a level of intelligence far beyond any other mammal.

Although the idea that our minds are a like a biological computer is useful, it has limitations. For example, how can patterns of neurons firing give rise to our sensation of a continuous flow of mental experiences? Nobody knows, as Steven Pinker puts it: 'Beats the heck out of me'. The metaphor for the mind as a computer does not explain consciousness. There are still many unknowns about how the mind works.

Differing levels of human intelligence

Psychologists have made some progress on the study of intelligence, however. All of the above mental abilities and more contribute to our intelligence, for example, learning, thinking, language, memory and imagination. Although every healthy human has these abilities, most of us have the sense that some people are more intelligent than others.

Despite the popularity of intelligence as a concept and the widespread use of IQ testing, there is no one widely agreed definition of intelligence. David Wechsler defines intelligence as: 'A global concept that involves an individual's ability to act purposefully, think rationally and deal effectively with the environment.'

The idea for testing intelligence came from Francis Galton, cousin of Charles Darwin. In 1905 French psychologists Binet and Simon built on his work and devised the first intelligence test. They used it in schools to identify children with learning disabilities.

At around the same time psychologist Charles Spearman found that when people are good at one mental task, they are often good at other types, and so proposed the idea of general intelligence, or 'g' as it is known.

One of the most popular intelligence tests for adults in use today was devised by David Wechsler in 1939. This tests your ability to think visually and verbally, your mental processing speed and your working memory abilities. The average score is set at 100.

130 and above:	Gifted
115–130:	High intelligence
85–115:	Average
70–85:	Low intelligence
70 and below:	Learning disability

A higher IQ predicts better school performance and the chances of having a high status job. Many studies have found that there is a link between a higher IQ and good job performance, so testing is widely used to select people for work.

You can test your own IQ at: http://www.iqtestexperts.com/iq-test/instructions.php

---

⚙ **brilliant** example

Too clever to be a cop?

Most recruiters are looking for a higher, not lower IQ, but in 1996, Robert Jordan discovered that his application to be a US police offer was rejected on the grounds that his IQ was 125. He was told that he was too bright and would therefore get bored and leave. His appeal on the grounds of discrimination was also rejected.

The US Army, on the other hand, rejects applicants with an IQ below 85. They found that recruits below this level went on to need more support and additional training than was justified by their contribution.

Although widely used, intelligence testing is controversial, with critics saying that it is a concept bound up with white, Western, male culture. For example, IQ predicts 'success' where success is defined as having a high status job; but perhaps another definition of success is raising happy children.

Are we getting more intelligent?

Whatever it is that intelligence tests measure, we are getting better at it. The IQ of the population has been rising since testing began. In the UK, the average IQ has risen by three points per decade. This is known as the Flynn effect, named after James Flynn, who brought the phenomenon to wider attention.

Intelligence tests have their scoring systems adjusted to keep the average IQ at 100.

Our intellectual abilities have not increased across the board – we are not much better at maths for example. Flynn points out we are better at tasks such as figuring out 'In what way are a dog and a rabbit alike?' This tests our ability to think in terms of abstract concepts. He theorises that one of the reasons is better education. At school we are encouraged to understand and grasp concepts, rather than memorise and rote learn facts. Steven Pinker goes further and suggests that it is our increasing ability to think in terms of abstract concepts such as fairness and justice that has helped us develop better capacity for moral reasoning which, in turn, has led to a decrease in discrimination and violence in society.

Presumably we can't continue to develop our mental capacities indefinitely, and the latest research shows that the Flynn effect may be coming to an end, at least in developed countries.

Could we all become geniuses?

We often equate the idea of genius with having an exceptionally high IQ. And we often assume that people like Einstein or Mozart were just born that way.

But psychologist K. Anders Ericsson argues that innate talent and IQ are not the most important factors in determining whether someone will show outstanding ability. Ericsson studied exceptional performers in different walks of life, such as doctors and musicians, and found that the most talented individuals were the ones who had worked hardest and longest. The ones with the most exceptional ability had practised their talent for at least 10,000 hours. It was not just the sheer length of

the most talented individuals were the ones who had worked hardest and longest time, but their determination to keep improving. Outstanding people are not content with their performance, but find ways to get better and better.

'It's not that I am so smart, it's just that I stay with problems longer.'

Albert Einstein

Other psychologists reject the idea of 'g' or general intelligence, arguing that it makes more sense to think of ourselves as having multiple intelligences, and wish to broaden the definition. Howard Gardner proposes that intelligence should also include additional abilities such as:

- Musical: the ability to detect pitch and tone, play an instrument, sing, compose.
- Bodily-kinaesthetic: the ability to use and control ourselves physically, such as in gymnastics and dance.
- Interpersonal: the ability to relate to others.
- Intrapersonal: the ability to understand yourself.

Social intelligence

Most people intuitively feel there is such a thing as 'social intelligence', the possession of 'people skills'. We recognise these skills as something many successful people possess, for example Bill Clinton and Oprah Winfrey. The concept of social intelligence is not new – it was coined by early psychologist Edward Thorndike, best known for his work on learning in animals.

brilliant definition

Social intelligence is: 'the ability to understand and manage men and women, boys and girls – to act wisely in human relations.'

Edward Thorndike, 1920

In 1976, psychologist Nicolas Humphrey proposed that it is our social abilities that make us intelligent as a species. He argued that it was not our increasing ability to solve practical problems such as finding food that drove the evolution of our big brains. Instead, it was the need to 'understand, predict and manipulate each other'. People who were more socially intelligent were better at getting others to cooperate with them, or at outwitting the competition.

it is our ability to be a 'natural psychologist' that made us intelligent

So according to Humphrey it is our ability to be a 'natural psychologist' that made us intelligent and gave us our big brains.

We tend to take living in social groups for granted, but getting along with other people is a complex task. To understand and predict each other's behaviour, we need to understand the contents of each other's minds, so we need to be able grasp other people's mental states, their beliefs, desires, intentions, emotions. This is called 'theory of mind' or 'mentalisation'.

We cannot understand or predict each other's behaviour without this ability. Simon Baron-Cohen explains why. Take this description of human behaviour: John walks around the kitchen, looks around and then leaves. Without using mental states, John's behaviour makes no sense: we have no idea what he is doing or what he is likely to do next. To understand John we have to talk about his mental states. If we say that John *wanted* to find something in the kitchen, but *forgot* what it was he was looking for and left, it makes sense.

Our ability to think in terms of mental states is so intuitive, that we use it for inanimate objects, too, such as 'my computer doesn't want to work'.

According to Steven Pinker this natural, everyday psychology for understanding other people's minds is the best system for understanding and predicting behaviour. He believes the science of psychology is never likely to improve on it. Our intuitive ability to grasp people's beliefs and desires is a better predictor of people's behaviour than any grand psychological theories, brain imaging techniques or psychological tests.

However, whether 'social intelligence' can really be measured accurately and used to predict behaviour is controversial.

exercise   What is your SIQ?

To obtain an estimate of your social intelligence, give yourself a score out of ten for how accurately each of these six statements describe you:

I am able to fit into any situation.

I have the ability to make others feel interesting.

I know what makes others tick.

I get on well with people I have just met.

I am good at sensing what others are feeling.

I know what to say to make people feel good.

Your total score indicates your 'SIQ' level:

0 10 20 30 40 50 60

Low social intelligence   High social intelligence

Whether tests like this are useful and meaningful in the world has not been established. But there is no doubt that much of our brain functioning is geared towards our social relationships and interaction. Psychologist and author Daniel Goleman has done much to make the idea of social intelligence popular. As he puts it 'our brains are mainly designed to connect to the brains of other people'.

If we see the mind as being adapted to understand other minds, an intuitive sense of the importance of emotions becomes apparent. This is the focus of the next chapter.

brilliant recap

- For many years psychologists studied only the links between our behaviour and the environment because they felt this was the only way to make psychology scientific.

- We share the same basic capacity for learning through classical and operant conditioning with other animals.

- Our minds can be understood as biological information-processing machines, and in some ways works like computers.

- Our level of intelligence is a result of our level of ability to process information in a way that makes us deal effectively with the environment.

- As well as solving practical problems, much of our brain functioning is geared to surviving as a social animal.

CHAPTER 2

Explaining
your emotions

The computer is a useful model for how the mind works, but clearly we do not coldly process information like a machine. Much of our mental life is made up of the sensations we call the emotions – we're all familiar with feeling highs and lows, such as the pleasurable anticipation of looking for a much-missed loved one in the crowd at the airport, and the pang of sadness when you discover they were not on the plane.

Do we even know what an 'emotion' is?

As yet there is no definition of 'emotion' to which everybody agrees. Most psychologists define an emotion as the experience of a subjective feeling, along with some physiological changes in the body, usually (but not always) accompanied by some outward signs such as a change in facial expression, body posture or tone of voice. Lastly, and most importantly, emotions are associated with carrying out a particular set of behaviours.

The advantage of having emotions

We often see our emotions as the enemy of calm, logical rationality. After all, emotion causes us to make rash decisions, such as that ill-advised outburst at your boss that ruined any chances of a pay rise. Have you ever wished you could be more coolly rational and run your life without being pulled and pushed in all directions by your emotions? Wouldn't you make better decisions without all this inner turmoil? Neurologist Antonio Damasio explored the answer to this question through his work with a patient called Elliot.

brilliant example

Elliot: The man who couldn't feel

Elliot's brain was damaged by a benign tumour and he had lost his ability to feel emotions. A professional man in his thirties, his intelligence, memory and all other intellectual abilities were completely unharmed, yet he was hardly able to function.

He could spend a whole afternoon at work trying to decide how to sort out a pile of documents, because he did not know whether it was better to put them in order of relevance, date or size. He was sacked from this job, then the next and the next. He couldn't make decisions – or he ended up making really bad ones. He lost his life savings on a project that everyone else could see was doomed from the start. He ended up having to live on disability benefits.

Rather than making decisions easier for him, having no emotions made his life and work much harder. Elliot couldn't make proper decisions because he couldn't 'feel' the value of different choices. According to Damasio, without emotions your 'decision-making landscape is hopelessly flat', meaning you are unable to prioritise or know what you want. Feelings are essential for guiding your behaviour, and not just in situations of high drama such as being threatened by a stranger with a knife, when fear tells you to run away. Emotions are important for decision-making in routine situations, such as deciding how to sort out a pile of papers.

Emotions make you focus on relevant problems and direct your actions. This is not to say that your emotions are always right – emotions can lead to bad decisions – but on the whole it is better for you to have them than not. For example, fear might make you jump out of the window of a burning house rather than carefully lowering yourself down with knotted sheets. But without fear you might not bother to get out of the burning house at all.

'The emotions aren't always subject to reason, but they are immediately subject to action.'

William James, psychologist, 1842–1910

Psychologists now believe there is no sharp distinction between physical feelings, like hunger, and the more subtle feelings that we call the 'emotions'. Both are feelings that direct you to do something that will further you or your family's survival. Hunger leads you to look for food. Anger makes you fight when people are trying to advance themselves at your expense.

Your emotions help you evaluate what is good or bad and what to do next. Elliot could not evaluate the differences between good and bad courses of action, because none had a good or bad 'feel'.

> your emotions help you evaluate what is good or bad

Which comes first, the emotion or the thought?

What exactly is the relationship between your thoughts and your emotions, and the physiological changes in your body? When you feel an emotion, is it because you have had a thought first? Or does emotion come first and change the way you think? Psychologists have debated these questions for over 100 years.

Early psychologists emphasised the role of the body. In the 1880s, William James and Carl Lange proposed that emotion is a result of physical responses. So if you see a bear, you get a rapid heartbeat and butterflies in your stomach, and because of these sensations you then experience the feeling called fear.

James and Lange believed that your different emotions have distinctive qualities because each emotion has its own pattern of physiological changes. For example, when you are angry your skin temperature rises, so anger is a 'hot' feeling. When you are frightened your skin temperature falls, so fear is a 'cold' feeling.

Profile: William James

William James (1842–1910) came from a wealthy, brilliant and well-connected family. He was brother to Henry James the novelist and Alice James the diarist. His family were associated with people such as Ralph Waldo Emerson and Henry David Thoreaux. William James was talented artistically, and originally intended to be a painter before he trained to be a doctor. He taught the first psychology course in America at Harvard, remarking that the first psychology lecture he ever heard was the one he presented himself.

Human emotion was just one of James' many psychological interests. He was deeply affected by problematic emotions himself. He was plagued by panic attacks and severe depression, and described how he spent all of one winter on the brink of suicide. He wrote a famous two-volume book, *The Principles of Psychology*, which is still widely read today.

James was inspired by Darwin and believed that human psychology was shaped by evolution, that we had innate human 'instincts' and a basic human nature. This view fell out of favour in psychology for many years as most people in the social sciences saw human beings as 'blank slates', shaped by experience alone. But over the past couple of decades or so, evolutionary approaches have become a mainstream part of psychology. As influential psychologists Leda Cosmides and John Tooby put it: 'William James's view of the mind, which was ignored for much of the 20th century, is being vindicated today.'

There is no doubt that changes in your body do play a part in the feeling of emotion. As common sense tells us, a surge of physical activity will change your emotions. It can work on an unnotice-able, subtle level – psychologists have discovered that your facial expressions do not just express how you feel, they can actually cause emotions. Research has shown that faking a smile actually creates a positive feeling – in one study people who held a pencil in their teeth, inadvertently causing a smile, found cartoons funnier than those who were holding a pencil in their lips, pre-venting a smile.

How does this work? The theory is that facial muscles send sig-nals to the brain about their position, and this tells you what emotion you are feeling. This is known as the 'facial feedback' hypothesis. This explains why Botox does not just make people look less emotional, they feel less emotional, too. Botox just freezes the face and does not affect the brain, yet women who have had Botox injections report feeling less emotional when watching funny or frightening video clips.

brilliant action

Try it for yourself

Test the facial feedback hypothesis. For about ten seconds, make yourself smile broadly, sit up straight and raise your chin. Can you feel your happiness increasing slightly? It may not work for you, but the effect is so marked for most people, that in one kind of psychological therapy, patients are trained to fake a 'half- smile' as a way of controlling their emotions.

The head or the heart?

Later psychologists began to emphasise the role of cognition. Schachter and Singer disagreed with the idea that emotion could be completely attributed to bodily changes. They believed that feelings depended on your *interpretation* of those bodily changes. If your heart begins to beat rapidly, what emotion are you feeling? If you are on a rollercoaster your brain will interpret it as excitement. If you are being confronted by a stranger with a knife your brain will interpret it as fear. Your cognitive appraisal of those same bodily sensations is different, and this is the key factor that determines how you feel. Two people experiencing identical bodily sensations on a rollercoaster will have different cognitive appraisals of those sensations, such that one person feels fear and the other enjoyment.

Psychologist Richard Lazarus developed the concept of cognitive appraisal further. He proposed that each emotion has its own characteristic pattern of meaning that you give to the relationship between you and your situation, what he calls 'core relational themes'. For example, in anxiety the interpretation you make is that you are facing a threat to your safety. He argued that your thinking patterns are so important in emotion that it is not necessary to have bodily changes in order to experience feelings.

brilliant example

Is thinking even necessary?

Imagine you have a phobia of spiders. You watch a video clip in which pictures of spiders flash onto the screen for 30 milliseconds – too quick for conscious awareness. Do you feel anxiety, despite having no conscious knowledge of seeing the pictures?

The answer is yes. It appears from research that the brain can react quickly from sensory input straight into the fear pathways in your brain (thalamus and amygdala), without involving the cortex at all.

So you can feel without thinking first, and bodily feelings can create emotions, yet cognitive interpretations of feelings are also important. Although the debate about thinking and feeling continues, many psychologists now agree that these interwoven strands cannot be unpicked. The subjective experience of emotion, physiological changes and cognition are all essential elements and it is not really possible to assign primacy to any one factor.

So is the debate in psychology about the differing roles of thought and emotion an artificial one? Probably – emotion and thought both involve processing information and they involve similar types of neural pathways. Analysing them as separate processes is just our common-sense way of understanding ourselves. Thinking from the heart really is no different from thinking from the head.

When emotions confuse us

How often do you feel confused by your emotions? Most people at some time or other have had the experience of being overwhelmed by emotions that are difficult to put into words. The richness and variety of words we have for different feelings is remarkable – there are over 550 terms for emotion in the English language.

One way psychologists have tried to make sense of this bewildering array of sensations is to try to reduce them into one set of basic emotions.

Charles Darwin began this approach, pointing out the similarities between how humans and animals express emotion. The facial expressions we show when disgusted or angry, for example, are almost identical to those made by other primates. His work sparked the idea that emotions can be seen as a set of survival mechanisms. In this view, an

> emotions can be seen as a set of survival mechanisms

evolutionary psychology approach, your emotions are like programmes guiding your behaviour in situations that are important to your survival and reproduction – from immediate challenges, such as finding food and avoiding predators, to long-term social challenges such as looking after your children, getting others to cooperate with you, warding off rivals for your loved one's affection, recognising enemies and spotting when you are being cheated. Emotions direct your attention to these essential matters and guide your behaviour towards solving them.

If this view is right, then it should be possible to identify a set of basic emotions, centred on different problems of survival and reproduction. Various theorists have proposed different lists of basic emotions. For example, Paul Ekman (one of the most well-known psychologists working in this area partly because of the detective series 'Lie to Me', which was inspired by his work) studied the facial expression of emotion in people all over the world, from Japan to Kenya to tribesmen and women in New Guinea. According to Ekman the basic emotions are:

Negative	Positive
Anger	Happiness
Disgust	Amusement
Sadness	Excitement
Fear	Sensory pleasure
Contempt	Contentment
Guilt	Satisfaction
Shame	Pride in achievement
Embarrassment	Relief
Surprise	Surprise

As you can see, surprise is in both lists – it can be positive or negative depending on the nature of the surprise. Ekman believes an astute awareness of how you are feeling, and how others around you are feeling, is likely to improve your functioning. If you are more attuned to feelings, you can understand and predict your own and other's impulses.

How good are you at reading other people's emotions? To find out, try taking the test at: http://greatergood.berkeley.edu/ei_quiz/

The first step is to be able to accurately name and recognise the basic negative emotions.

The eight negative emotions

The negative emotions have been studied the most in the past, so there are clear definitions and many studies on why they occur.

1 Anger

What was the last thing that made you angry? The chances are that it was another person – someone who deliberately showed no concern for your welfare, showed you no respect or had no regard for fairness. As a social animal, one of the problems you face is that other people may harm or cheat you in order to advance themselves, so you need to have a mechanism to make you take action in these situations. It is anger that moves you to fight for your own or your family's rights – it evolved because it promotes your welfare in situations of conflict of interest.

brilliant insight

Although obviously anger can have destructive and damaging consequences, anger works. A study by Tiedens found a display of anger helped people get their own way in a negotiation. Showing signs of anger can give the impression that you are dominant and have high status, in other words it can get you more 'respect'. The same researcher also found that people were more supportive of Bill Clinton when he was showing anger over the Monica Lewinsky affair, than when he was expressing sadness.

It is important that you recognise signs of anger in others to alert you to the danger of being attacked. Your brain can process signs of anger automatically and quickly without any cognitive effort. Paul Ekman says you can even detect the signs of anger in others before they are conscious of it themselves. For example, you can notice a slight thinning of their lips or an 'edge' to their voice.

brilliant insight

Have you ever accused someone of getting annoyed, but they completely deny it? Of course, they may be lying, but there is a good chance that you have spotted their anger before it has registered in their own awareness.

2 Disgust

This is the emotion that motivates you to avoid contaminated, harmful or noxious substances, such as rotting food, faeces, body fluids or other potential carriers of disease. The function of disgust is to help you avoid harm or infection. It has an easily recognised facial expression of a wrinkled nose and raised upper lip.

brilliant example

Within the last minute you probably swallowed some saliva, a normal process that does not disgust you.

Now spit into a glass of water and then drink it. Does the prospect feel disgusting? Would you drink juice that has a sterilised cockroach in it? Would you eat chocolate that is shaped like dog faeces?

Psychologist Paul Rozin has conducted various experiments like this in the name of research. Most people refuse to drink their own spit - it seems that once saliva has left our body, it becomes an alien and disgusting body fluid and our emotional response against it is activated. Intellectual knowledge about sterilisation cannot conquer disgust against cockroaches.

Small children are happy to do these things, however, and Rozin argues that disgust as an emotion normally develops between the ages of four and eight.

However, the emotion of disgust is not just limited to inanimate objects. We also respond with disgust towards people we feel are strange, diseased, unfortunate or morally contaminated. Paul Ekman found that people were far more disgusted by the thought of a morally repugnant behaviour, such as paedophilia, than the thought of eating someone else's vomit. The feeling of disgust is an important influence on your interpersonal behaviour, causing you to turn away from or avoid the person or people who disgust you.

Sherman and Haidt scanned students' brains and showed them pictures of people from different social groups. When the students looked at pictures of the homeless or drug addicts, this activated the region of their brain associated with disgust.

3 Sadness

This is the emotion you feel as a response to the loss of something, such as a possession, a relationship or a person. At one end of the spectrum there is the momentary sadness when you lose a favourite pen, at the other extreme is your grief at the loss of a loved one. It is the price we pay for having social bonds – when they are broken we experience the emotional pain of sadness.

Biologist Lewis Wolpert says sadness motivates us to find the lost desired object or person, or to try to replace what has been lost. The facial expression of sadness, the tears and hunched posture, is a social signal which should, if you are fortunate, move someone to come to your aid.

brilliant insight

One of the most painful aspects of being human is that our superior powers of imagination, abstraction and anticipation give us an extraordinary capacity for feelings of loss. We not only feel sadness in response to real losses, but to future or imagined ones. People who have a child with a disability grieve for the healthy child they never had; people who look in the mirror and see the first grey hair feel sad about their lost youth; rejected contestants on reality TV talent shows weep for their lost 'dreams'.

A famous example of extreme sadness was Queen Victoria. She was 42 when her husband Prince Albert died, and she never really recovered from this loss. She withdraw from public life for years, refused to wear a crown, and wore a widow's bonnet and dressed in black for the rest of her life.

4 Fear

Fear is the emotion that has been researched the most. It is the feeling that moves you into action when you are under physical or social threat.

Fear concentrates your mind on the most important survival issue of the moment. If your loved one is out late and you are worried about their safety, you will find it difficult to concentrate on anything else. Your mind will keep wandering back to this concern, and you won't be able to concentrate on less important matters, such as reading the paper or watching the television. If the situation continues, fear will spur you into action and you will give them a call or start a search.

The physiological component of fear is recognised by everybody: the muscle tension, pounding heart and sweating. These are the body's preparations for exertion, known popularly as the 'flight or fight response'.

But your behavioural response to fear is more subtle than this. When your boss tells you that your job is under threat you don't (usually) run out of the building screaming. Fear helps you to take whatever swift action is necessary, including covering up the fact that you are frightened. Fear does not usually cause people to 'lose control' and make silly choices, fear concentrates your mind so you choose the best option, whether it is snatching your child out of danger, freezing to avoid attracting the attention of a predator, or smiling calmly so your enemy does not sense you are afraid.

Fear has a characteristic facial expression – eyebrows raised and drawn together, tensed lower eyelids and lips stretched horizontally – because signalling fear to others can be a useful survival tool. In situations where you think you might be in danger, you automatically scan the faces of people around you. If you see fear on other people's faces, you can use this information to take quick action, without waiting around to work out the danger for yourself.

brilliant tip

Are you afraid of public speaking? Many people count it as among their biggest fears. But why? It's not physically dangerous, but we think it's *socially* dangerous. We think the audience will evaluate us badly, that we risk losing status, being shamed or rejected. For a social animal, this is a threatening prospect. In ancient times, if you were ejected from your social group, you would probably have died.

However, our social fears are misplaced. So many people are frightened of public speaking that much of the audience is made up of people who feel for your predicament – and rather than judge you badly they tend to elevate your social status in their minds thanks to your bravery in taking the stage. A stumbling, nervous performance can evoke social acceptance and support, drawing you closer to the group.

▶

So the next time you have to give a speech, remember that the common fear will help you, not harm you.

5 Contempt

According to Ekman, contempt is the emotion you experience when you feel vastly superior to someone, a sensation of greater moral superiority, power or status. Unlike disgust, contempt is not something you would feel towards an inanimate object, it is about the evaluation of other human beings. It is the emotion you feel when you assign a lack of social value to others.

This emotion is characterised by the curling lip and sneer, and the raised chin with the accompanying impression that you are 'looking down your nose' at someone. It is always unpleasant to be the object of contempt, but Ekman believes that although they might not admit it some people enjoy feeling contemptuous towards others. He suggests that people insecure about their status will particularly relish this feeling.

6 Guilt

Guilt is the emotion connected with responsibility. It is the unpleasant sensation you have when you believe that you may have harmed or neglected others or yourself through your action or inaction. It is an important emotion in motivating us to care for each other and ourselves. Guilt guides you into engaging in nurturing or altruistic behaviour.

guilt guides you into engaging in nurturing or altruistic behaviour

According to psychologist Richard Lazarus, guilt is the result of breaking a moral rule. So you feel guilty for eating a cake when you were trying to lose weight, or guilty for not helping your child with her homework because you were watching TV instead.

There is no characteristic facial expression or body posture for guilt, you can only indirectly infer guilt by looking for other signs of emotions such as shame or anxiety.

Of course, not everyone is compelled by the same feelings of guilt – if everyone had the same sense of guilt there would be no need for the legal system. People who hardly experience guilt at all are likely to engage in antisocial or criminal behaviour, and one of the defining features of the psychopath is that they are incapable of feeling guilt. The psychology of the psychopath is explored in more depth in Chapter 4.

7 Shame

According to psychologist Paul Gilbert, shame is the feeling you experience when you believe yourself to be unacceptable as a person. You feel shame when you have attributes you believe will cause you to be rejected or 'put down' by others. These attributes could be physical such as body shape or size, or personality traits such as being 'boring' or unacceptable acts you have committed such as lying or stealing.

What is the social function of shame? Paul Gilbert believes that shame is the emotion that is important in making us tend to form social hierarchies. Some people are more dominant or high-ranking than others, and shame is the feeling you experience when you have lost 'rank'. The behaviour associated with shame is to try and hide the aspect of yourself you are ashamed of so others do not find out and cause you to lose social standing.

8 Embarrassment

Paul Gilbert says this is the feeling that you have done something that reduces you in the eyes of others, but is limited to your behaviour in a particular situation, such as knocking over your coffee cup. It does not result in you feeling you are totally unacceptable as a person.

Do negative emotions outweigh positive emotions?

Positive emotions are just as important in understanding ourselves as the negative ones. These positive emotions are easy to recognise – most people intuitively understand them quite easily. For example, relief is a pleasurable feeling when a negative emotion subsides, usually accompanied by a sigh. Unfortunately for us, there are more basic negative emotions than positive ones, probably because survival depended upon us taking swift, focused action. Negative emotions narrow your attention and actions. In contrast, positive emotional states tend to broaden your focus and encourage you to be playful and explore.

Positive emotions have not been studied by psychologists as much as the negative ones, although this is changing, and there is now a branch of psychology called 'positive psychology', focusing on the study of happiness. Chapter 10 will go into more depth on positive emotions and the psychology of happiness.

Of course, although we experience these emotions as positive, this does not mean they are positive for others, for example criminal offenders often feel pride, enjoyment and satisfaction in perpetrating antisocial acts.

Complex emotions

In Ekman's view all our other emotions, such as love and jealousy, are combinations of the basic positive and negative emotions. Other psychologists disagree – for example, some see love as a basic emotion, because research suggests falling in love is the same experience for all of us, whatever our sex, age, race or sexuality.

The complex emotion we know as the feeling of 'hatred', the emotion that drives people to violence, is thought to be a blend of anger, contempt, disgust and fear. Disgust is a particularly significant part of dehumanising others, enabling people to commit atrocious acts. People who are objects of hatred are referred to as 'filth' or 'scum'. During wartime, opposing sides try to engender feelings of disgust towards the enemy, for example, in the Second World War the Japanese were portrayed in propaganda materials as rats. The complex emotions of hatred and love are addressed in more depth in Chapters 6 and 7.

brilliant example

An FBI researcher studied speeches made by world leaders and heads of ideologically motivated groups involved in conflict with each other. He analysed these speeches for emotional content. He discovered that verbal expressions of anger, contempt and disgust in their political speeches predicted acts of aggression and violence soon after.

The problem of emotion

Humans have a particular problem with regard to emotion. Because you can reflect on the contents of your mind, you can evaluate what is in your consciousness. This means that you can have emotions about your emotions. These are known as 'secondary emotions' because they are emotions about your 'primary emotions'.

For example, you may be so afraid of being overwhelmed by feelings of loss that you avoid feeling them altogether and delay the grieving process. Or you may be ashamed of your feelings of fear, and hide them, leading to feelings of loneliness and isolation. Some therapists believe that the phenomena of having feelings about our feelings is the root of many of our emotional difficulties.

> having feelings about our feelings is the root of many of our emotional difficulties

🏃 **brilliant** action

Many of us have difficult or tangled emotions and have been through experiences that leave us feeling upset or traumatised. Social psychologist James Pennebaker discovered that the simple act of writing down our feelings has a powerful effect. He conducted research where he asked people to write about their deepest feelings for 20 minutes on three occasions over a few days. Most people found this exercise upsetting or difficult at the time, but they showed long-term benefits afterwards, including greater well-being, better immune functioning and better health. It is not clear why this works, but somehow the act of writing helps us express and process our emotions in a way that is beneficial.

Here are the instructions for the Pennebaker exercise if you wish to try it:

> 'Over the next four days, I want you to write about your deepest emotions and thoughts about the most upsetting experience in your life. Really let go and explore your feelings and thoughts about it. In your writing, you might tie this experience to your childhood, your relationship with your parents, people you have loved or love now, or even your career. How is this experience related to who you would like to become, who you have been in the past, or who you are now?

> Many people have not had a single traumatic experience but all of us have had major conflicts or stressors in our lives and you can write about them as well. You can write about the same issue every day or a series of different issues. Whatever you choose to write about, however, it is critical that you really let go and explore your very deepest emotions and thoughts.'

Empathy

An important part of our emotional lives is our ability to experience empathy. Psychologist Simon Baron-Cohen (cousin to the comedian and actor Sacha Baron-Cohen) proposes that there are two types of empathy. The first is 'cognitive empathy', the ability to recognise other people's feelings and mental states. The second is 'affective empathy', the ability to respond to someone else's mental state with the appropriate feeling. For example, cognitive empathy enables us to recognise someone's distress, and affective empathy is feeling sympathetic and wanting to help. Cognitive and affective empathy are vital in anticipating each other's needs and play an important role in our caring and altruistic behaviours, such as looking after our children and giving to charity.

brilliant example

Is empathy just a human trait?

Would you give an electric shock to people you know? How about if you were starving and could only get food by giving fellow humans electric shocks?

In 1964 Masserman wanted to find out if animals also have the ability to recognise and respond to another's distress. He experimented on whether monkeys would rather go without food than pull a chain that delivered an electric shock to fellow monkeys.

He discovered they were reluctant to do so, and their reluctance was stronger for monkeys they knew than strangers. One monkey starved himself for 12 days rather than give his companion a shock.

Simon Baron-Cohen believes our capacity for empathy lies on a spectrum, with highly empathic people at one end, and people who have 'zero degrees of empathy' at the other. These are the individuals we recognise to be evil and cruel, criminal psychopaths such as Ted Bundy.

The discovery of mirror neurons

Italian neuroscientist Rizzolati found neurons that fire both when a monkey is carrying out an action and when watching another monkey carry out the same action. At the time many people believed that the brain mechanism for empathy had been found, but now most see mirror neurons as just one part of the system. Simon Baron-Cohen believes the circuits involved in empathy involve ten different areas of the brain.

How empathic are you?

Give yourself a score out of ten for each of these items, then add up your score:

I feel others' emotions.

I anticipate the needs of others.

I reassure others.

I make others feel good.

I am concerned about others.

I make people feel welcome.

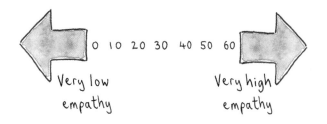

0 10 20 30 40 50 60

Very low empathy   Very high empathy

For a fuller assessment of your capacity for empathy, go to: http://glennrowe.net/BaronCohen/EmpathyQuotient/EmpathyQuotient.aspx

> your emotional intelligence, or 'EQ', may be more crucial to your success in life than your IQ

Emotional intelligence

The ability to feel empathy is one aspect of 'emotional intelligence'.

There has been huge public interest in this concept, much of it generated through the work of psychologist Daniel Goleman. He argues that your emotional intelligence, or 'EQ', may be more crucial to your success in life than your IQ.

brilliant definition

Emotional intelligence is: 'the ability to monitor one's own and others' feelings and emotions, to discriminate among them and to use this information to guide one's thinking and actions.'

Salovey and Mayer, 1990

Emotional intelligence is part of social intelligence. Our ability to deal with emotions is part of our overall skill in dealing effectively with other people. But critics say there is no convincing evidence that emotional intelligence is linked to job performance and financial success and leadership, as Goleman has claimed.

However, there is no doubt that severe difficulty in recognising and regulating emotions in yourself and others is a central part of many human problems, such as psychological disorders, abusive parenting and many types of criminal conduct. A low EQ is associated with substance abuse and criminal behaviour.

What is your EQ?

Give yourself a score out of ten for each of these six questions and add up your score:

I think about the causes of my emotions.

I am usually aware of the way I am feeling.

I notice my emotions.

I often stop to analyse how I am feeling.

I find it easy to show others I care about them.

I listen to my feelings when making important decisions.

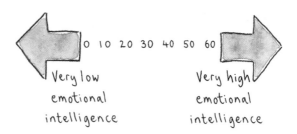

0 10 20 30 40 50 60

Very low   Very high
emotional   emotional
intelligence   intelligence

You can also try the test of emotional intelligence at: http://personality-testing.info/tests/EI.php

Emotion is difficult to study, given the subjective nature of the experience. But psychological research into emotion is now flourishing, with new disciplines emerging such as 'affective neuroscience', the study of brain processes involved in emotion. Once a topic relatively neglected in psychology, it is now recognised that emotion is central to the functioning of our minds. Developing insight into emotions is one of the keys to understanding yourself and others.

brilliant recap

- Emotions are an essential part of decision-making.
- Thought and emotion are not two separate phenomena – they both involve processing information and have similar neural pathways.
- Emotions evolved as programmes which guide your behaviour to solve problems of survival and reproduction.
- Many of our basic emotions are centred on our relationships with others.
- There are probably a set of basic emotions that all human beings share.
- The ability to identify emotions in yourself and others and your capacity for empathy are vital to your social functioning.

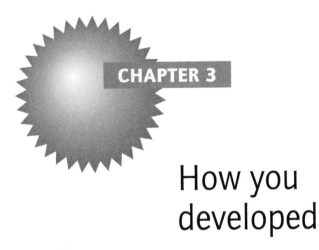

CHAPTER 3

How you developed

Your emotional and intellectual make-up was determined by your unique pathway through life. Understanding how we develop as children has always been a big focus in psychology. More recently, our development has been studied as a life-long process, as we change through the whole course of our lives.

Psychology of the newborn

Human beings begin in a peculiarly helpless state. We have a limited behavioural repertoire at birth, for example, the rooting and sucking reflex and crying. Compared to other mammals, we are born before our brain and body are complete. If we stayed in the womb for the same proportion of the life cycle as other primates, we would be born at the age of 18 months. But we come into the world early because our head size is so large that a later birth would be physically impossible.

Do babies learn while in the womb? Perhaps, in a limited way. An experiment was devised whereby newborns could suck on a pacifier that activated either a recording of the mother's voice or a stranger's voice. They activated the familiar voice recording more often, implying they had learned the sound patterns they heard in the womb. But there is no evidence that playing music or foreign languages to unborn babies will give them any advantage.

Although we are pretty helpless, we are not born as 'blank slates' as seventeenth-century philosopher John Locke believed. Your genes equip your brain with a set of programmes, which unfold actively throughout your development.

we are not born as 'blank slates'

For example, we have some cognitive abilities at birth. Newborn babies can tell the difference between simple shapes such as crosses, circles and triangles. They are born with a preference for looking at faces: newborns follow a picture of a face with their eyes rather than look at a picture of a jumbled up face.

What about recognising emotions? Newborns can distinguish between happy, sad and surprised expressions. They can also imitate a facial expression, such as opening their mouth wide or sticking their tongue out.

Within a day, babies can distinguish between their mother and a stranger, even if the stranger has similar colouring and hairstyle. Babies very quickly show a preference for looking at their mother.

brilliant insight

Looks matter

Babies have large eyes, a high forehead and a small nose, which elicit the 'aaahh' reaction and our nurturing instincts. Their cute appearance is one of the survival mechanisms which help ensure we will look after them. And it may be that it is best to be as pretty a baby as possible: studies show that mothers of more attractive babies pay more attention to them. Mothers of less attractive babies look at, play with and touch them less often.

We tend to blame the media for our obsession with beauty and physical perfection, but even newborn babies prefer to look at more attractive faces. We start judging people on the basis of looks from birth, a somewhat depressing thought.

The importance of bonding

Babies survive through the bond with a caregiver and this is a key part of the baby's psychology. From about seven months, babies form a distinct preference for their mother over other people and are wary of strangers. Psychologists originally believed this bond formed because they associated their mother with food.

In 1969, Harlow and Harlow devised a series of heartless experiments to study the behaviour of infants. They separated baby monkeys from their mothers at birth, and instead they were given a choice of artificial structures to cling on to. One 'mother' was made of bare wire, the other made of a soft cloth.

Harlow and Harlow discovered that the babies preferred the cloth mother, even when it did not dispense any milk. The baby monkeys used the cloth mother for a sense of safety. They were willing to touch frightening objects if they kept hold of the mother with a hand or foot. It was this research and his work as a child psychiatrist that inspired John Bowlby to propose his famous 'attachment theory'.

Attachment is the basic biological drive babies and children have to stay near the mother. The closeness gives babies a sense of safety and security from which to explore the world. The child's development unfolds within this relationship. If this bond is disrupted then Bowlby believed there would be severe consequences for the child's emotional, social and even intellectual development.

'Mother love in infancy is as important for mental health as vitamins and proteins are for physical health.'

John Bowlby

According to Bowlby, your attachment with your mother gives you an 'internal working model'. This is a cognitive and emotional representation in your brain of you, your mother and the relationship between you both. This internal working model guides how you relate to other people, for example, it will influence the quality of your adult love relationships.

brilliant insight

Why do abused children love the parents who treat them cruelly? In the past, people were puzzled about the fact that children were often strongly attached to their abusive parents. Harry Harlow investigated this by giving baby monkeys 'abusive' mothers – cloth structures that fired random blasts of cold air. Far from being put off, the monkeys seemed even more desperate to cling on to the 'abusive' mothers.

It is now recognised that infants' drive to form an attachment is so strong, they will attach to the person who provides their care, almost no matter how neglectful or sadistic they are. Abusive parents often wrongly believe that because their child is attached to them, this means their parenting is good enough. Bowlby says that attachment is a primary drive, like hunger. Just as the starving will eat unpalatable food, a child will love the most abusive of parents.

How childhood attachment impacts the rest of your life

Mary Ainsworth, a colleague of Bowlby, discovered that there were different distinct patterns in the quality of the attachments between babies and mothers.

Secure attachment

Secure attachment is where the child feels safe with the mother and uses the security of the mother as a base to explore the environment. They are distressed if the mother leaves, but on her return they seek contact with her and are easily comforted and quick to settle. Around 65 per cent of children fall in this category.

Insecure attachment

1 Insecure-avoidant: The child explores the environment but does not want to be near the mother, turning away or avoiding eye contact with her. They treat strangers and the mother in a similar way, perhaps even preferring the stranger over the mother. During a reunion with the mother after a separation, they take little notice of the mother, and are as easily comforted by a stranger as their mother.

2 Insecure-resistant: These babies are reluctant to explore the environment, preferring to be with the mother. They show extreme distress on separation from their mother, but when she returns they are not easily comforted and may have a tantrum or are difficult to settle.

3 Insecure-disorganised: This category of attachment was added by Main and Solomon. These are infants who don't show the above clear patterns, but appear to have a lack of coherence in their response. They may seem to both want to be near the mother but to avoid her, too – such as walking towards her with the head turned away. During the reunion they show disturbed or confused behaviour, such as rocking, freezing or fearfulness.

As you probably guessed, secure attachment is associated with better development and adjustment in children, such as higher self-esteem, more perseverance, higher curiosity, more positive emotions, fewer negative emotions and more advanced cognitive development. Securely attached children typically have healthier romantic relationships as adults. The way you relate in adult love relationships will be influenced by the type of attachment you had as a child, explored further in Chapter 7.

> secure attachment is associated with better development and adjustment in children

Your childhood attachment style may even determine what kind of attachment your own children will have to you. In a study of expectant mothers, Peter Fonagy found that the attachment style the mothers had experienced themselves predicted the type of attachment their babies would have to them in 75 per cent of cases.

The most worrying time of attachment is the 'insecure-disorganised' type. It is associated with child abuse and alcoholism or mental illness in the mother. Children with this type of attachment are more likely to have behaviour and psychological problems in later life.

the way you are treated as a child actually affects the brain's physical structure

The latest research in neuroscience shows that the way you are treated as a child actually affects the brain's physical structure; lack of adequate emotional care prevents the brain from developing properly.

brilliant tip

Look for attachment styles in children. How can you tell if a child has an insecure attachment? It is not the amount of distress a child shows when the mother leaves that matters. Children show different levels of distress at separation, depending on their temperament. Instead, to judge the quality of a mother and child's relationship, look at the child's reaction to the mother after the *return* from a separation. If the child avoids the mother, or is very difficult to settle, or shows confused, disturbed behaviour, they may have insecure attachment.

Why are some children insecure?

The answer is thought to be about the ability of the mother to respond appropriately to the baby's needs. If the parent is responsive, the baby forms a secure attachment. Mothers who can accurately identify the baby's feelings and desires are more likely to have a secure child.

However, if the parent is not attentive or sensitive enough, the baby forms an insecure attachment. Mothers who are likely to have insecure babies ignore emotional cues or respond inappropriately, such as trying to play vigorously with the baby when he is tired, or speaking sharply to her when she is frightened. Typically, the mother's behaviour towards the child is more about satisfying her own needs, for example, giving the child a cuddle when she wants to be comforted herself, rather than attuning to what the baby needs.

brilliant insight

Many of us continue to yearn for a stronger and wiser figure throughout our lives. Our attachment needs do not necessarily go away just because we are grown up. When we realise our parents are not all-knowing and all-powerful, we may look for someone or something else to fulfil this role, particularly in times of stress. So we try to find another source of security. This is why many of us are vulnerable to charismatic figures who appear strong and able to guide us through life. Substitute attachment figures could be a leader, the government or even God.

Your attachment to these substitutes might help make up for inadequacies in your earlier relationships. For example, it's been suggested that some people who have an insecure attachment to their parents can compensate by having a particularly secure relationship to God.

How you developed your social and emotional intelligence

According to attachment theory, these abilities develop through your relationship with your caregiver. Your mother helped you understand and label your emotions and mental states. As part of everyday life your parent responded to you verbally and non-verbally and helped you make sense of what you were experiencing inside. A simple example is that if you were fractious through lack of sleep, she would say 'you are tired', and help you settle down and go for a nap. Over time you learn to recognise the feeling of tiredness yourself and you know that you need rest.

Through these types of interaction, you developed a better awareness of your own mental states: your feelings, thoughts, needs and desires. Thus we learn to control our impulses, manage our emotions and soothe ourselves.

So it is through the attachment relationship that we learn to 'mentalise' or develop 'theory of mind'. Understanding our own and other people's minds is an essential part of being a well-functioning human being.

But as Peter Fonagy and Anthony Bateman theorise, when a parent cannot accurately recognise the child's feelings, thoughts, beliefs and desires, then the parent cannot help the child develop them. A mother who has a good ability to mentalise might, for example, see that her child is frightened, and say 'Don't be scared, you are safe' and calm them down. A mother who is poor at mentalising might say 'Don't be naughty' and punish them.

The ability to mentalise is part of emotional and social intelligence. If you had good enough care, you will have developed the ability to understand and regulate your own emotional response, and from this foundation you will have learned to recognise the emotions of others.

> The ability to understand and regulate emotions is an important predictor of future behaviour

Research shows that children who are hard to manage and have behaviour problems typically have poorer emotional understanding. The ability to understand and regulate emotions is an important predictor of future behaviour. One study found that preschool children who couldn't control their feelings when given a disappointing gift were more likely to show disruptive behaviour in later childhood.

brilliant example

Waiting for an extra marshmallow

The ability to control our impulses is an important part of development. In the famous 1972 'Stanford marshmallow experiment', Walter Mischel gave four-year-old children a marshmallow, and said that if they waited 15 minutes before eating it they could have an extra one.

Children younger than four are usually unable to wait – their immediate emotions are overwhelming and take priority over everything else. But by four most children are able to regulate their impulses. A minority ate the marshmallow straightaway, most tried to wait but then succumbed to temptation, while about a third delayed gratification and waited long enough to win the extra marshmallow.

A follow-up study found that the children who controlled their impulses went on to have better psychological adjustment and better grades as teenagers. Forty years later, in 2011, some of these subjects were tracked down. Their level of impulse control was still relative to their childhood level, suggesting that this remains a pattern for life.

Early theory of development

Many of the early ideas on child development were based on Freud's theories. He believed that adult problems could always be traced back to childhood events.

Freud believed that our development is governed by the instinctual desire to get pleasure (what he calls the libido) and that we pass through stages where the source of pleasure changes. His theory was that problems in moving from one stage to the other cause problems in later life. His stages were:

- Birth to one year: Oral – source of pleasure is the mouth and sucking.
- One to three years: Anal – pleasure and focus is on controlling anus and defecating.
- Three to six years: Phallic – the genitals are the erogenous zone, boys have sexual feelings to mother (Oedipal complex), girls to father (Electra complex), but fear retribution from their other parent.
- Six to puberty: Latency – sexual desire goes into a resting phase.
- Puberty onwards: Genital – sexual feelings re-emerge.

However, many of Freud's ideas about development are unscientific in that they are difficult to prove or disprove. The above ideas that have been tested have been unsupported, and there is no evidence for his Oedipal or Electra complexes.

Yet Freud's theories caught the popular imagination and remain influential to this day: people still think psychology is about analysing our subconscious urges to marry our mother. Freud's biggest contribution in this area was probably that he pointed to the importance of early childhood in affecting our later lives, rather than the above specific ideas.

Profile: Sigmund Freud

Sigmund Freud (1856–1939), the Austrian neurologist and founder of psychoanalysis, is one of the most controversial and well-known figures in the history of psychology. He was the favourite son of ambitious parents, and critics of Freud say that his need for fame eclipsed any regard he had for scientific rigour. For example, early in his career, after just a few weeks of experimenting with cocaine including taking it himself and giving it to his friends, he wrote a paper extolling its virtues as a medicine. He pronounced that cocaine was a cure for all sorts of complaints, including morphine addiction. He later distanced himself from these claims. Freud later developed psychoanalysis, the first 'talking cure' and influenced many, but was fiercely protective of his theories, rejecting people who questioned his ideas, such as his former best friend and 'disciple' Carl Jung.

Freud spent the last year of his life in London, having fled Vienna in 1938 because of the rise of Nazism. He was in danger of persecution and his daughter, Anna Freud, also a psychoanalyst, had been interrogated by the Gestapo. Freud, aged 82, and very ill with mouth and throat cancer, was unable to arrange a rescue for his four sisters and they all died in concentration camps. The mouth cancer, a result of his famous fondness for cigars, caused him immense pain, and so he asked his personal physician to hasten his end and he died of an overdose of morphine.

Freud's legacy, like the man himself, is controversial. He was the founder of psychotherapy and many of his insights have stood the test of time. But his theories have also caused unnecessary suffering. His belief that children have unconscious sexual desires for their parents meant that over the years many young victims of sexual abuse had their pleas for help dismissed as 'fantasy'. Conversely, the Freudian idea that people 'repress' traumatic memories has led to therapists 'uncovering' false memories of child sexual abuse, resulting in the incarceration of innocent men.

Today, Freud continues to divide opinion. Many see him as a great man who has made an invaluable contribution to our understanding of ourselves, while others see him as the purveyor of a damaging and destructive pseudoscience.

Watching how children develop their intelligence

If a child's care is good enough, both emotionally and physically, their cognitive abilities will develop. Understanding everyday life requires learning a huge quantity of knowledge – basic common sense consists of millions of facts – and one of the most intriguing parts of psychology is discovering how children achieve this daunting task. The way it unfolds has been much studied, but there is still controversy and disagreement in the field.

Jean Piaget was one of the most influential people in this area. He saw children as active agents in understanding the world. He believed thinking developed in four stages, each one building on the last.

1 Birth to two years old

Piaget called this the 'sensorimotor' stage of development, when infants develop their knowledge of the world through their senses and motor actions. At this stage of development infants focus on discovering the relationship between actions and consequences. The child is actively interested in seeing what happens when they do different actions, such as pushing a bowl off the table. In this way they discover the laws of cause and effect.

Until nine months, babies are unable to form a mental representation of an object that is out of their sight. If you hide a desirable object from a baby younger than nine months, they will not look for it – they are unable to hold objects in the mind. At about nine months they will know it has gone somewhere and look for it, a development known as object permanence. Is there a link to the question of why attachment in infants does not begin until seven months? Bowlby thinks so: babies develop object permanence for their mother and can now represent her existence in the mind when she's not physically present.

brilliant tip

Put a cloth over a toy. Does the baby appear to immediately lose interest? If so, he or she has not developed object permanence yet.

2 Age two to seven years

Piaget called this the 'preoperational' stage. At this age, the mental representation of objects goes beyond the here and now of a toy either visible or under a cloth. A child begins to think using symbols, can understand that words stand for something else, and so is able to use words. This mental representation means that they can engage in 'pretend play', for example pretending a doll is a person.

However, children at this stage cannot 'operate' on information very well – their skills for manipulating and transforming information are weak. An example is mentally 'undoing' something in their head. You can test a young child on this ability, by pouring water from a wide glass into a tall glass and asking them which glass holds more water. They will say there is more water in the tall glass, because they can't mentally undo the process of pouring the water back into the short glass and realise it is the same.

According to Piaget, children are also egocentric at this age – they don't understand that other people have different viewpoints.

3 Age seven to eleven years

This is what Piaget called the 'concrete operational' period. Children can now manipulate and transform information about practical, concrete concepts. They can classify objects and place them in logical order – for example, they can sort their books by size, author or the colour of the cover, recognising there are multiple aspects to things.

At this age they lose most of their egocentrism – but Piaget thought they may not be very skilled at viewing things from another's perspective.

They are better with practical questions and problems than with abstract concepts, and prefer to solve problems in highly practical ways rather than through mental reasoning. For example, they use trial and error, or guess at a solution and then test it, rather than determining the best actions mentally. If you watch an eight-year-old on a computer using unfamiliar software or a new game, you will observe constant activity as they try out different buttons or menu choices.

So their abilities have advanced but they are still 'earthbound, concrete and practical minded' thinkers.

4 Age eleven and older

Piaget called this the 'formal operations stage'. Adolescents are able to think in abstract terms, they are no longer tied to thinking about concrete objects that exist in the natural world. They can form a mental hypothesis via logical reasoning and are able to deduce a solution to a problem without physically trying alternatives.

Try asking children the following question: 'If mice are bigger than cats, and cats are bigger than whales, which animals are the biggest?' Under-elevens struggle with this, because they use concrete information and find it hard to ignore their practical knowledge of whales and mice. Older children, though, can keep to the strict mental logic and answer the question, enjoying the mental game of ignoring reality.

Adolescents are curious about abstract questions. They can think about things like injustice and free will, grappling with abstract questions such as the meaning of life.

Was Piaget right?

Later research reveals that how our thinking develops is more complicated than this. For example, object permanence happens much earlier than Piaget believed. In one study, five-and-a-half-month-old babies were shown impossible scenarios, such as a cardboard rabbit that appeared and disappeared in an impossible way. They stared at impossible scenarios for longer than possible ones, implying they have a sense that objects have an existence even when unseen.

Piaget thought all adolescents reach the 'formal operations' stage. However, this underestimates the variability of human abilities – some do not think well in abstract ways and this lasts into adulthood.

One of the most important questions is how we learn to understand the world from another person's perspective. Piaget thought under-sevens were egocentric, unable to see from inside the head of someone else. This is now known to be untrue: from an early age most children can understand differing perspectives.

The importance of perspective for understanding the mind

One study found that children as young as 18 months old have this ability. They were tested to see their reaction towards an adult person who had their possessions taken away or destroyed by another adult. The toddlers showed concern towards the other person – they had grasped something about another's mental state.

The development of 'perspective taking' allows children to attribute mental states to others – beliefs, desires, intentions and emotions. As a social animal, having a mind with the ability to understand and predict what other minds do is a vital part of being human.

The ability to understand other people's minds may even have its own special brain circuitry. Simon Baron-Cohen proposed that the inability to comprehend other people's minds – what he calls 'mind blindness' – is the problem underlying autism. People with autism have specific difficulties in managing social interaction.

Most children though have the ability to take other people's perspectives of others and love to explore this through pretend play. When you see a small child pretending to be a cat, or a princess, or a policeman, they are developing their mental ability to understand the minds of others.

The importance of play

Lion cubs play by hunting one another, stalking and pouncing. Not only does this develop physical skills but it is important for their mental development. Likewise, children's pretend play is often about pretending to be at a later stage of life, such as playing at being parents or doctors or teachers.

Just as physical play has obvious functions in developing the body, pretend play helps develop the mind, stretching children's cognitive, emotional and intellectual capabilities. Although children engage in fantasy play, they know the difference between fantasy and reality from an early age. For example, one study found that from about age three onwards, most children can reliably distinguish between real and imaginary cookies.

Influential Russian psychologist Lev Vygotsky argued that children learn our social rules through imaginative play. When children pretend to be other people, they learn to understand the rules that govern our social lives. For example, a child playing at shop is not only learning about abstract concepts such as money, but about the roles of customer and shopkeeper. A child giving a tea party to teddy bears is learning about norms of behaviour as a host. Research shows that children who engage in pretend play according to social rules at nursery are more likely to follow classroom rules when they go to school.

The next time you watch children playing, look out for them applying social rules and see whether they project imagined mental states onto objects or toys. Also observe whether they talk to themselves. Vygotsky emphasised the importance of language as a tool in helping children develop. Preschool children in particular talk to themselves when solving problems, carrying out tasks or playing. He believed children use language to help themselves – 'private speech' helps them organise behaviour, and children who do this are better at problem-solving tasks. As they get older, the private speech becomes whispers and then lip movements before stopping altogether and presumably becoming private inner speech. Language appears intertwined with the developing human mind.

How children develop language

Our ability to represent information with words and exchange them with others is one of things that makes us so successful as a species.

As mentioned in Chapter 1, famous linguist and thinker Noam Chomsky believes that different languages all have the same underlying features – what he terms 'universal grammar'. For example, all languages have nouns and verbs. Most theorists now believe that babies have an innate capability for language, hardwired into the brain.

The sequence of language development is very much the same in all cultures. It begins with single words for people and physical objects and at the age of one children have a handful of words. By the age of two it has become sentences of two or three words. Grammatical sentences are used by three-year-olds and by the age of four a child will be using adult-like sentences. Steven Pinker points out that language develops in the same sequence, despite differing exposure to language early on, for example, people in some cultures don't speak to children directly when they are infants.

An important clue to language is that if you are not exposed to it before the age of six, you never grasp it properly. It appears that the brain's capacity to recognise word order and rules in language has a critical period from birth to six.

Steven Pinker presents the example of Chelsea: a girl who was born deaf and misdiagnosed as being 'retarded'. Her deafness was not discovered until she was 31, when she was finally given hearing aids. She managed to learn how to function independently, but her language never developed properly. She lacked the instinctive understanding for syntax and word order, for example, she would say things like:

The boat sits water on.

The woman is bus the going.

Breakfast eating girl.

Combing hair the boy.

 insight

Words, words, words

Human beings have an incredible capacity for language. At 18 months, most children have a vocabulary of about 25 words. It is about 15,000 by age six – learning about ten words a day. By age 17, most people know about 60,000 words, the equivalent of learning a new word every 90 minutes of our lives.

Social factors in development

Lev Vygotsky emphasised the importance of other people in children's development. This was in contrast to Piaget, who saw them as acquiring their abilities relatively independently. Vygotsky's view is that interacting with adults or older siblings who have greater abilities helps children advance their cognitive and social understanding.

Psychologist Judith Harris points to the importance of peers in our social development. Children learn from children their own age as well as their elders. Who has the most effect on our development – parents, siblings or friends? Judith Harris controversially argues that our peer relationships are the most important influence. She points out that when a family locates to a new area, children will copy the accent of their new peers, not that of their parents. Moreover, she argues that the chances of being involved in juvenile crime depends on the kind of peers you have, not the kind of parents you have.

How do brothers and sisters affect you?

According to popular belief, the birth order of children shapes your personality. People believe that the older child is more successful, the younger child is spoiled and rebellious, and the middle child is confused and neglected. They point to anecdotal evidence – for example, 21 out of the first 23 astronauts in space were firstborns. But this effect might be due to family size and wealth. Astronauts are more likely to come from wealthier, better educated families with few children, so successful children from these families are more likely to be firstborn.

There is much debate in psychology about the effect of siblings, and no consistent findings. The finding that seems to be most reliable is that the more older brothers a boy has, the more likely he is to be gay. This is thought to have a biological basis, as it holds true even when boys are adopted by other families with no other male children.

What about the effects of being an only child? The idea in psychology that being an only child has a negative effect on personality was started by Alfred Adler, who worked alongside Freud for a while. According to Adler, being an only child 'is a disease in itself'. However, this belief has not been borne out by research. The only difference between only children and those with siblings is that only children have a higher desire for achievement. This may be because parents have more time and resources to devote to them.

Being the parent of a teenager: what impact do you have?

Research shows that parenting styles do have an impact on children's development. For example, studies of teenagers and their parents show the effect of different styles. According to Diana Baumrind, there are two important types of behaviour in parents:

- How responsive they are: how they react to a teenager's needs in an accepting and supportive way.
- How demanding they are: how much they ask of the teenager.

Parents vary along both these dimensions, thus there are four basic styles:

1 Authoritative: parents are highly responsive and demanding. Authoritative parents are warm and supportive, yet also offer guidance and have clear expectations about acceptable behaviour.

2 Authoritarian: low in responsiveness, but highly demanding. They are not warm or supportive towards the adolescent, but enforce high standards of behaviour and expect obedience without question.

3 Indulgent: highly responsive, but low on demandingness. Interact with warmth, but are passive about directing the adolescent's behaviour, giving them lots of freedom.

4 Neglectful: low on both responsiveness and demandingness. These parents are not particularly interested in their adolescents. They spend minimal time and energy on them.

The best outcomes are achieved by authoritative parents. If your parents had this style, you are more likely to be self-reliant, successful in school, self-controlled, creative, curious and adaptive. In contrast, authoritarian parenting styles are associated with teenagers who are less socially skilled, less confident and curious. Indulgent parenting results in teenagers who are less mature, less responsible, have

> the best outcomes are achieved by authoritative parents

lower leadership ability, and are more influenced by peers. Finally, neglectful parents are likely to have teenagers who are impulsive, show delinquent behaviours and engage in early sex, alcohol and drug use.

Adolescence: struggle and exploration

In 1905, G. Stanley Hall proposed that adolescence is a time of turmoil and since then psychologists have characterised adolescence as a stormy process.

Erik Erikson, who was originally inspired by Freud before forming his own ideas, theorised that during adolescence we struggle to find a sense of identity, and at this age we do not know who we are or where we are going in life. The task for adolescents is to form a stable sense of who they are. They experiment with different ideologies, values and lifestyles before they find one that gives them a sense of coherence and direction.

Adulthood: continual development

Erikson's view is that our development continues throughout adult life, and we struggle with different dilemmas at different stages. He saw development as a process of finding our way successfully through these dilemmas or, as he put it, achieving 'psychosocial tasks'.

So in early adulthood, age 20 to 24, the dilemma is whether we should have an intimate sexual relationship and share our lives or remain independent. Our previous development will help determine this, for example, whether we have developed the ability to trust others. In middle adulthood, from our twenties to sixties, the task is working out what our contribution will be to society, for example, through having children or work. The dilemma in this is the tension between making a contribution versus satisfying our immediate desires. At age 65 we look back and assess our lives. If we have resolved the earlier dilemmas of life well enough we should enter old age with a sense of satisfaction.

So there are multiple influences on your development, and the person you are today was shaped by the complex interplay of the above factors and more. How has your personality turned out? This is the question of the next chapter.

brilliant recap

- We are not born as blank slates, we have innate mental programmes for developing our cognitive, emotional and social abilities.

- Our emotional and social development is affected by the type of emotional care we received in childhood.

- The way we relate to others is influenced by our early attachment relationships.

- Play and peers and learning from others are an important part of our development.

- Parenting style - authoritarian, authoritative, indulgent or neglectful - shapes children's behaviour.

- Psychological change continues through adulthood.

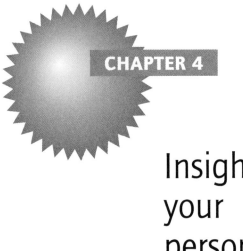

CHAPTER 4

Insight into your personality

'Character is destiny.'

Heraclitus, Greek philosopher, 540–480 BC

We all make judgements about our own and other people's personalities, using labels for ourselves like 'outgoing', or 'shy', or 'aggressive'. Sometimes these perceptions are accurate and useful in understanding and predicting people, sometimes they are not. What can psychology add to our common-sense understanding of our individual differences?

In the 1920s Gordon Allport was one of the first psychologists working in this area and made the term 'personality' popular. Hans Eysenck was one of the pioneers of rigorous research into personality and was the psychologist who discovered many of the basic findings.

brilliant definition

Personality is: 'A dynamic organisation, inside the person, of psychophysical systems that create the person's characteristic patterns of behaviour, thoughts and feelings.'

Gordon Allport, 1961

To try to understand personality, Allport and Odbert analysed the 18,000 words we use to describe our behaviour and reduced these words into a smaller set of basic traits. After decades of studying the results from questionnaires and refining the traits even further, psychologists such as Lewis Goldberg found that much of our behaviour can be described in terms of five basic factors. These are known as the 'Big Five': Agreeableness, Conscientiousness, Neuroticism, Openness and Extraversion.

The 'Big Five' personality traits

1 Agreeableness

Before you read about this trait, rate each of these six items out of ten for how accurately they describe you:

I have a good word for everyone.

I believe others have good intentions.

I respect others.

I accept people as they are.

I make people feel at ease.

I do not insult people.

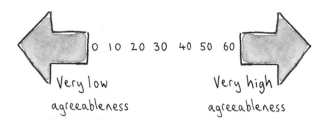

If you are high in agreeableness, you place a large importance on the needs of others. You find it easy to strike up rapport and tend to trust people. You typically have harmonious relationships and are slow to anger so rarely 'fall out' with people. When you do, you are quick to forgive.

An advantage of high agreeableness is that you benefit from having good relationships and reap the rewards of cooperation. High agreeableness has a downside though – you might find other people 'walk all over you', or that you have sacrificed you own needs for others. Agreeableness is a trade-off between cooperating with others and having more of a competitive style.

People low on agreeableness are generally more interested in advancing their own interests, rather than fulfilling the needs of others. They are less friendly, do not trust so easily and are less responsive to other people's distress. They are more likely to be non-compliant and hostile. People low in agreeableness come across as antagonistic and cold-hearted to people who have high agreeableness. But having low agreeableness can be an advantage. A study of business executives showed that the less agreeable they were, the more their income and the higher their rank in the company. Low agreeableness also predicts success in other competitive areas such as the creative industry.

Psychologist Daniel Nettle believes the key to this trait is your level of empathy – he calls people with high agreeableness 'empathisers'.

2 Conscientiousness

Out of ten, how accurately do these statements describe you?

I am always prepared.

I pay attention to details.

I get chores done right away.

I carry out my plans.

I make plans and stick to them.

I do not shirk my duties.

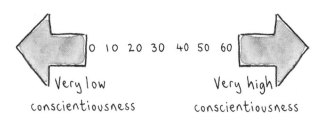

0 10 20 30 40 50 60

Very low
conscientiousness

Very high
conscientiousness

If you are high in conscientiousness, you are good at planning and deferring gratification in order to achieve a longer-term goal. Conscientious people set a lot of goals and stick to them. They tend to be tidy and organised.

There are advantages to this trait: conscientiousness predicts success in work and studies. Conscientious people live longer, probably because they are more scrupulous about looking after themselves and are less likely to engage in risky, impulsive activities such as addictive behaviour. A disadvantage of conscientiousness is that sometimes it pays to be spontaneous and switch plans. People with this personality trait can become overly preoccupied with orderliness and control at the expense of fun and leisure, and may be more vulnerable to obsessive behaviour.

People low in conscientiousness are more 'laid back'. Striving is not important to them, they tend to be less tidy and organised and more spontaneous. Low scorers set fewer goals for themselves and don't stick to them. They see people high in conscientiousness as austere, inflexible and petty. People very low on conscientiousness will struggle to focus and stick with tasks. They may have a problem with impulse control. People very low on this trait are more likely to have addictions or display antisocial behaviour.

Conscientiousness is the balance between impulsive spontaneity and planning. According to Daniel Nettle, people with high conscientiousness can be summed up as 'controllers'.

3 Neuroticism

Do these statements sound like you?

I often feel blue.

I dislike myself.

I am often down in the dumps.

I have frequent mood swings.

I panic easily.

I get stressed out easily.

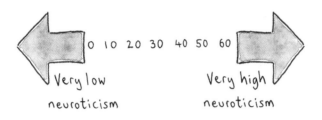

0 10 20 30 40 50 60

Very low neuroticism   Very high neuroticism

If you are high in neuroticism, you experience more negative emotions, such as anxiety, low mood, sadness and anger. This can be an advantage – negative emotions exist for a reason. They have evolved to make us avoid the harmful things in life like physical danger, loss or social ostracism. Possessing more negative emotions causes you to see threats, so you will err on the side of caution and keep yourself safe. High neuroticism can give you more motivation. Students who are neurotic, when this is combined with organisation and discipline, get better university results.

> high neuroticism can give you more motivation

High neuroticism can also be an advantage in that it gives you a more reflective mindset. One study showed that people high in neuroticism are particularly successful in professional jobs that require higher levels of thinking. The downside is that neuroticism means more suffering, and more vulnerability to depression and anxiety.

People low in neuroticism are calmer and do not get stressed easily. As they are less sensitive to danger they take more risks, which can be an advantage because at times reward comes from risk. It can also be an advantage in some jobs. People low in neuroticism are suited to police and military work; they cope well with danger and threat and can coolly deal with the problem in hand. People who choose dangerous activities are likely to be low in neuroticism, for example, Everest climbers. The disadvantage is that low neuroticism makes you ignore real danger: about one in fifteen Everest climbers die during their climb.

Nettle sees neuroticism as the balance between being sensitive to threat and not sensitive enough. People with high levels of this trait are 'worriers'.

4 Openness to experience

How do you score on this trait?

I believe in the importance of art.

I have a vivid imagination.

I carry the conversation to a higher level.

I enjoy hearing new ideas.

I enjoy having wild flights of fantasy.

I get excited by new ideas.

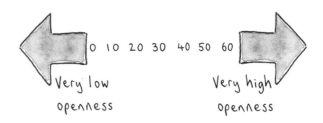

This characteristic is about your openness to creative thinking and new ideas. If you are high in openness, your mind works in a divergent way, making connections between different concepts and coming up with original angles. Because of their divergent thinking, people high in openness tend to challenge social norms. They typically enjoy art, poetry and literature and tend to be liberal in their outlook. They are drawn to artistic or creative professions, tend to defy convention and take their own path through life such as frequent changes of career. Their creativity gives them an advantage in attracting partners.

The downside of having high openness is that creative minds are more vulnerable to unusual beliefs. Nettle believes that because people high in openness have fewer boundaries between different parts of their mind, this makes them more vulnerable to mental illness. Openness predicts creative activity, but also contact with psychiatric services. There are high rates of mental illness among writers and artists.

People low in openness prefer tradition and staying with the familiar, and are less interested in exploring new ideas. They tend to have a conventional approach to life with a more conservative outlook.

Openness is the balance between creativity and tried and tested wisdom. Nettle calls people high in openness, 'poets'.

> openness is the balance between creativity and tried and tested wisdom

5 Extraversion

You may already have a fair idea of where you fit on this scale:

I am the life of the party.

I feel comfortable around people.

I start conversations.

I talk to a lot of different people at parties.

I don't mind being the centre of attention.

I warm up quickly to others.

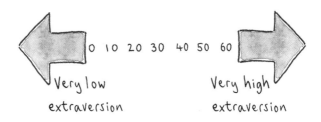

0 10 20 30 40 50 60

Very low
extraversion

Very high
extraversion

This is the best known personality dimension, first made popular by Carl Jung. Most people know extraverts are usually outgoing and gregarious. But what makes them this way? Hans Eysenck proposed that the difference between extraverts and introverts is an inherited difference in brain physiology.

Psychologists believe extraverts experience more intensely positive feelings than introverts and so are more responsive to rewards. This means extraverts are more likely to gravitate to the 'good things in life': achievement, love, sex, excitement and human company.

Although extraverts enjoy being with people, note this does not mean they are more socially skilled than introverts. Extraverts will enjoy going to parties, but they might talk loudly about topics nobody else is interested in, offend people and flirt with everyone in the room, leaving a trail of resentment. How well people get on with others is not determined by extraversion, but by agreeableness.

Research shows extraverted men and women have more sexual partners than introverts. And because extraverts are highly driven by rewards, they are more easily tempted to be unfaithful. Extraverts have more affairs, and more multiple marriages, so have more divorce and family breakdown.

Extraverts are more willing to explore and take risks in their search for rewards. This will sometimes pay off, but more risks means more accidents. Research shows that people who have car accidents have higher extraversion scores.

Introverts are much less driven by external rewards, they do not get such a kick out of the pleasures of life, but they are more dependable.

Extraversion is about how much reward should be pursued in relation to the risk. Nettle says people high in extraversion can be summed up as 'explorers'.

Profile: Hans Eysenck

Hans Eysenck (1916-1997) is another controversial figure in psychology. His parents were both actors and he was born and brought up in Germany. When Hitler came to power, Eysenck was told he could not go to university unless he joined the Nazi Party. Eysenck was opposed to Hitler and all he stood for so he left Germany and settled in England.

Eysenck investigated many subjects, but is best known for his work on intelligence and personality. He said he was an extreme introvert, who found it difficult to talk to new people and speak in front of an audience. He believed there was a strong inherited component to personality, at a time when people thought that all behaviour was learned, so his ideas were unwelcome and treated with suspicion. But he was unafraid of controversy and was an outspoken critic of others, including Freudian psychotherapists, whom he considered to be unscientific and ineffective.

He also believed there was a strong genetic component in intelligence and angered people by speculating that there were genetic differences in intelligence between the races. His critics accused him of right-wing racism, and he was punched in the face by a woman during a talk at the London School of Economics. He also received

▶

death threats against himself and his children. Despite these accusations, Eysenck maintained that his experiences as a young man in Germany had made him vehemently opposed to any kind of oppression based on race or anything else.

Eysenck was one of the founders of behaviour therapy, a prolific researcher and author of over 100 books. His son Michael Eysenck also became a prominent psychologist and is a professor at Royal Holloway, University of London.

Is there a sixth trait: honesty-humility?

Some psychologists believe honesty-humility does not fit into the 'Big Five' traits and should be added as a sixth. This is about our level of sincerity, fairness, avoidance of greed and modesty. You can estimate how you might score on this by looking at fairness, one aspect of the honesty-humility trait:

I would never take things that are not mine.

I would never cheat in my taxes.

I return extra change when a cashier makes a mistake.

I would feel very bad for a long time if I was to steal from someone.

I try to follow the rules.

I would regret my behaviour if I were to take advantage of someone impulsively.

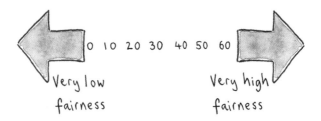

0 10 20 30 40 50 60

Very low fairness

Very high fairness

People who are high in honesty-humility treat other people with great integrity and are reluctant to promote their own interests over others. Low scorers on this trait are more likely to show antisocial and vengeful behaviour, get into trouble at work for stealing and absenteeism, and are more likely to be unfaithful to their sexual partners.

Does your personality change over time?

Your personality is probably more fixed than you think. One study found people's Big Five scores stayed similar, whether they were tested again in six days' time or twelve years' time. Over adulthood, people do change slightly, for example, we tend to become more agreeable and conscientious and less neurotic.

your personality is probably more fixed than you think

Although it is difficult to change your basic personality type, you can change the way you express it. So if you are an extravert who loves skydiving, but your family and friends complain it is too dangerous, you might be just as happy switching to another exciting but less dangerous hobby, like mountain biking.

Understanding your own personality can help you make choices more effectively. If you want to work with people, and you are high in agreeableness, something in the caring professions would suit you better than a sales or managerial job that required you to stand your ground and make tough decisions. Of course, it is not always realistic to make sweeping changes in career even though you have realised you are not naturally suited to your job. For example, because of economic realities, there are plenty of people high in openness stuck in routine jobs where original thinking is frowned upon. If this is you, then it is important for you to have a creative outlet in your spare time.

Gauging other people's personalities accurately will help you predict their behaviour and give you realistic expectations for change. You can set yourself up for frustration and disappointment if you try to persuade your boss, friend, child or partner to change their basic personality type to suit you.

> gauging other people's personalities accurately will help you predict their behaviour

brilliant tip

Watch out for the small details

When trying to figure out someone's personality, it can be useful to pay attention to the details of their behaviour. Sometimes people show their personality in the smallest of ways. For example, you go to a restaurant on a date and notice they rearrange the knives and forks and salt and pepper, in effect organising the table. This could reflect an overall trait of conscientiousness. Or you notice that your date frowns at the waiter for accidently spilling a drop of wine, a small give-away of their overall low agreeableness. Nettle says small behaviours like this are like fractals, a pattern in miniature which, when you look at it close up, is similar to the pattern the person shows as a whole.

A different approach to personality: your basic desires

Psychologist Steven Reiss takes a different approach. He believes personality is best understood in terms of our motivations.

Reiss asked thousands of people from different walks of life about what drives them most, and he concluded that humans have 16 basic desires. The individual profile you have in terms of these 16 determines your personality. Read this list. Which desires are most important to you? Rate them as important to you, neutral for you or not important for you.

Power – the desire to have control and influence over others. People with this desire are highly ambitious, strive for leadership roles and are dominant in social situations.

Independence – the desire to be free from reliance on others. People high in this desire dislike advice from others, like being on their own and hate depending on other people for anything.

Curiosity – the desire for understanding and knowledge. If you ask lots of questions, enjoy the quest for truth and spend a lot of time in thinking and reflecting, then this characteristic applies to you.

Acceptance – the desire to be socially included. People who desire acceptance have an intense dislike of rejection and criticism, and need other people's approval to feel good about themselves.

Order – the desire to be organised. People who desire order like planning, cleanliness and clear rules.

Saving – the desire to have things. Saving is part of your character if you collect things, are careful with your money and frugal in your habits.

Honour – the desire to abide by the moral code of your parents, culture, religion or nation. This characteristic is important for you if you place a high value on principles, duty and loyalty.

Idealism – the desire for a fairer society. People high in this trait are willing to make personal sacrifices to give to the needy or volunteer for good causes.

Social contact – the desire to spend time in other's company. Do you hate being by yourself and need to be around people most of the time to be happy?

Family – your desire to have and look after your own children. People with this trait feel having children is central to their happiness and spend more time with them compared to other parents.

Status – your desire for social prestige. This trait refers to people who always want to buy the best, have or do things to impress others, and strive to be a member of a prestigious group.

Vengeance – the desire to get even. This is the extent to which people like to compete with others and seek revenge for harm or insults. People with a high desire for vengeance show more anger and aggression to others.

Romance – the desire for sex and beauty. A high desire for romance is characterised by spending a large amount of time engaging in or looking for romance, sex or beautiful things.

Eating – desire for food. If you are high in this desire you spend a lot of time either eating or dieting.

Physical activity – desire to exercise. Is playing sport and physical activity important to you and something that has been part of your whole life?

Tranquillity – the desire for calmness and emotional stability. People who need tranquillity are easily frightened and have low tolerance for stress.

Reiss believes most, if not all, of these basic desires are found in animals in a different form. For example, animals have curiosity, they will investigate new objects, and many engage in saving by hoarding food.

He believes all your actions are directly or indirectly aimed at satisfying these desires. For example, what motivated you to read this text? Was it 'curiosity', the desire for understanding and knowledge? Or perhaps it was because you wanted to impress someone with your knowledge, the desire for 'prestige'.

Maybe you wanted to understand yourself better because you want more inner peace, more 'tranquillity'.

Reiss says understanding your own and others' unique pattern of motivations can help you have a more satisfying life. We should look at our basic desires and change our circumstances so they can be better fulfilled.

'When you awaken each day, your desires start to influence your behaviour automatically. They prod you to do what you do. When you satisfy them you gain value-based happiness, which is a deep sense that your life has purpose and meaning.'

Steven Reiss

Understanding other people's basic desires can help us to allow others to be themselves. It is a doomed quest to make them more like us. For example, if your partner has a low level of curiosity, no amount of conversation about interesting books or tickets to fascinating talks is going to make them develop a hunger for knowledge if the desire is just not there.

brilliant timesaver

Never-ending arguments

Do you often have the same old argument with someone in your life? Is it because you have different basic desires?

According to Reiss, no amount of reasoning, arguments and fighting is going to change someone's mindset. For example, fighting is common between couples when one person has a high desire to save and the other does not. If Reiss is right, the 'saver' is never going to persuade their partner that it's a good idea to put money in a high interest account rather than blow it all on a dream holiday. They might as well stop wasting their breath and solve the problem another way. In this situation, the couple need to recognise that

▶

they have different basic motivations and will have to work out some way of managing it together. One option would be to reach a compromise position whereby both have their desires partially fulfilled, such as going on a more modest holiday and banking some of the money.

Do you hate the thought of being put into 'boxes'?

You might feel an instinctive resistance to being categorised in one of the above ways. Our personality is our individuality, and it's a little bit soul-destroying to have it reduced to a psychologist's grid of traits or desires. Are we really so easy to label and place in boxes?

Many psychologists now believe it does not make sense to try to categorise people's personalities by coming up with a list of traits. Walter Mischel points out that people's behaviour can vary, depending on the circumstances. People do not behave consistently across situations. For example, you might be organised and conscientious at work, but have a chaotic home life.

> it makes more sense to try to understand people's unique 'behavioural signatures'

He argues it makes more sense to try to understand people's unique 'behavioural signatures' across different situations.

Mischel believes personality is defined by the way you see a situation, your abilities, your expectations of yourself and others, your values and your ability to plan and regulate your behaviour. This approach is called 'social cognitive theory'.

So while it may be useful to categorise personality, it can also pay to notice your own and other people's unique patterns and the differences in the way people react in different circumstances. For example, some people might have a strong need for power at work, but are happy to take a back seat at home.

exercise   Understand yourself

It's hard to take personal criticism. But a good way to gain insight into yourself is to think about the personal criticism you have had over the years.

Do people say you are too bossy, too passive, too quick to judge, too disorganised, too exacting, too lazy? Most people's instinct is to feel the criticism is unjust, defend themselves vigorously and try to forget the criticism. But if the same comments have occurred more than once – and you can bear to think honestly about them – it is likely you can learn from criticism.

Daniel Ofman is a management consultant who has developed a useful tool intended for understanding personality at work but also relevant for our personal lives. According to Ofman, most negative qualities can be seen as an excess of a good quality. For example, if people criticise you as being too exacting, this could be because you have an excess of a good quality – you have very high standards. According to Ofman, every positive quality has a 'pitfall'. In other words, too much of a good thing is a bad thing. Examples of good qualities and their pitfalls are:

- Hardworking? The pitfall is you may become a workaholic.
- Assertive? The pitfall is you may become too bossy.
- Relaxed? The pitfall is you may become too lazy.

Suppose you realise that you are a person with high standards. Being too exacting will be your pitfall. You can also predict that you will have a dislike of sloppiness and will feel particularly negative towards people with your opposite quality. Ofman calls this your 'allergy'. You will be likely to clash with people who have qualities you are 'allergic' to. Your challenge is to be more realistic in your expectations of others

▶

You can plot it out on a table like this:

Positive quality:	Pitfall:
High standards	Too exacting
Allergy:	**Challenge:**
Sloppiness	Realistic expectations

As an exercise, create four-quadrant diagrams, one for each of your main traits. Start by identifying your positive qualities – for example, are you caring, hardworking, assertive, well-organised, relaxed. Then try to fill in any other section of the quadrant. If you have something you are particularly 'allergic' to, a trait you really dislike in others, then fill in this quadrant and try to work back to consider which positive quality it relates to. Are there pitfalls that you fall into by being too excessive about a positive quality?

By filling in the quandrants you can predict the problems that might arise between you and other people. If you can anticipate yourself clashing with someone, you can prepare for it. Understanding why a clash occurs shows where compromise might be found. This exercise can require the investment of time and a great deal of honesty, but it will give you more insight into yourself and others.

People you simply can't like: the Dark Triad

Most of us try to get along with others, even if they have a personality trait we don't like. We make compromises to avoid conflict and accept we can't expect to like everyone we meet, and some are not going to like us. Usually we reach a place where we are happy enough with some aspects of an acquaintance or work colleague, while other aspects we dislike.

But what about those people who you just can't stand? And those who seem charming at first, but about whom later you realise they have hidden their unpleasant traits? In our personal lives we can move away from these people – ending friendships or avoiding them socially. But in our working lives we might be forced to be with them for hours a day, trapped with them in an office or a classroom in college.

We are all likely to struggle with people who have the personality traits known as the 'Dark Triad': Machiavellianism, narcissism and psychopathy. People with these personality types are very low in agreeableness and are low in the honesty-humility trait. The three Dark Triad personalities have overlapping similarities: they are all selfish, dishonest, cold-hearted and aggressive.

1 The Machiavellian personality

You start working with a new manager at your office. You soon realise she is a self-interested schemer who manipulates others to achieve what she wants. She lied to you about a project and is deceitful with customers; you've heard her charming the managing director while ignoring a junior manager. You discover she is shameless in telling people what they want to hear, always calculating relationships to her own advantage.

You have just met a Machiavellian personality. Such personalities are cynical, believing that, like them, everybody else in the human race is selfish and deceitful. Their main interest is in achievement, power, money or winning. Machiavellian characters often make marvellous villains in fiction – J. R. Ewing in the TV series *Dallas* is a classic example – but they are no fun to work with.

The risk they pose to us is that we will be double-crossed, cheated, lied to or cast aside when our usefulness is over. Our main defence is to be forewarned – we cannot change their personalities but we can mitigate the effects of their behaviours. Machiavellian personalities can climb to the top and become powerful leaders or military dictators, but people with this personality are found everywhere. Many people have Machiavellian traits to a mild extent. To find out the extent of yours go to: http://personality-testing.info/tests/MACH-IV.php

2 The narcissistic personality

On your university course you meet a man who, at first, impresses you with his confidence. He is sure of his future success and expects wealth to come his way. From his descriptions of his abilities and the important demeanour he presents, you think he is someone more special than most. But then you notice how he loves the admiration of others and how he always seems to think he's entitled to special treatment. He constantly tries to associate with people of high status and one day he lets slip that he thinks everyone else is envious of his talent and good looks. When one student doesn't treat him with respect, he gets furious.

This is the narcissistic personality. Like Machiavellian personalities narcissists see other people as a means to satisfying their own desires, but with the additional trait of an inflated opinion of themselves. They have grandiose ideas about themselves, and fantasise about incredible success, wealth, fame or ideal love. The typical response to anyone who doesn't treat them how they think they deserve is outbursts of anger. An example of a narcissistic character is David Brent in the TV series *The Office*. People in the entertainment industry, such as actors or celebrities, tend to have higher levels of narcissism than the general population, but you will meet narcissists in every walk of life.

If you come across a narcissistic personality, recognise they will have little interest in your needs. Any relationship with them will be based on you serving them and their ego. And if you try to deflate their deluded self-opinions this is likely to backfire and just make them furious with you.

Many of us have at least some level of narcissism, to find out yours you can go to: http://psychcentral.com/quizzes/narcissistic.htm

3 The psychopathic personality

What would you notice if someone with a psychopathic personality arrived at your workplace? Very probably you would notice nothing at all.

Psychopaths can fool experienced experts: Robert Hare, a psychologist who created the standard tools for measuring psychopathy and works with the FBI, admits he himself has been taken in by them. They can put on great personal charm and are found at every level of society and in every profession – there are psychopathic teachers, doctors, lawyers and psychologists. The popular view of the psychopath is that of the mentally deranged serial killer. This is not accurate – a psychopath is not mentally ill and may or may not be a killer. Most are not murderers. Robert Hare says the psychopath we are most likely to encounter is the smooth talking swindler who expertly separates us from our hard-earned cash.

Psychopaths are like narcissists, using people for their own ends and having an inflated opinion of themselves, but they have another characteristic that makes them more destructive. They feel little emotion and have no empathy. A psychopath does not feel distressed by someone else's distress.

'Psychopaths are social predators who charm, manipulate and ruthlessly plough their way through life, leaving a broad trail of broken hearts and shattered expectations.'

Robert Hare

Robert Hare outlines the defining features of psychopathy:

Emotional/Interpersonal

Glib and superficial

Egocentric and grandiose

Lack of remorse or guilt

Lack of empathy

Deceitful and manipulative

Shallow emotions

Social deviance

Impulsive

Poor behavioural controls

Need for excitement

Lack of responsibility

Early behaviour problems

Adult antisocial behaviour

About 20 per cent of people in prison are psychopaths. More than half of all serious crimes are committed by them; their lack of normal emotion and empathy means they are unconcerned about harming others. A notorious example is the serial killer Jeffrey Dahmer. But most are not in prison, and as all personality traits are on a continuum, many of us will show at least some psychopathic features.

To find out where you fit on the psychopathy scale, an online questionnaire is available at: http://personality-testing.info/tests/LPS.php

Snakes in suits

The majority of psychopaths are not murderers or criminals, but are ordinary people in ordinary jobs. Because psychopathy is so common, we are likely to encounter at least one psychopath in a typical day, according to psychologists Paul Babiak and Robert Hare. Psychopaths can rise high in society because of their manipulative ways and unfeeling ruthlessness.

Babiak and Hare, in their book *Snakes in Suits: When Psychopaths Go to Work*, say that the modern corporate world is the ideal environment for ambitious psychopaths. Their charisma, eagerness to take charge and willingness to rattle cages can make them appear to be the perfect person to come into an underperforming department and shake up the status quo.

But psychopaths can do a lot of damage in the workplace. Their deceit, manipulation and self-serving ways will cause a trail of destruction. If you are unlucky enough to have a psychopathic boss, they will play on your weaknesses to exploit and even bully you. Other people will find it difficult to believe because of their charm and charisma. Babiak and Hare say that if your life is being made a misery at work by a psychopathic boss, then ultimately the best option for you might be to find another job.

So personality is an important part of understanding ourselves and others, and to a certain extent we can predict behaviour by assessing our individual traits. But looking at the individual only takes us so far – we also have look at the influence of other people.

brilliant recap

- A large amount of the variation in our behaviour can be described in terms of six basic personality traits.
- Most personality traits are a 'trade-off' with advantages and disadvantages at both extremes.
- A useful way of understanding personality is to get insight into your basic motivations from the list of 16 basic desires.

- People also have their own unique 'behavioural signatures' across different situations.

- Trying to change someone's personality is unlikely to be successful – it is more realistic to look at ways to work with it.

- There are three extremes of personality to watch out for: Machiavellianism, narcissism and psychopathy, the 'Dark Triad'

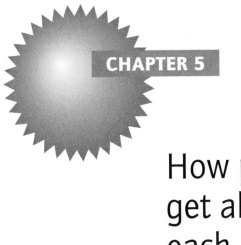

CHAPTER 5

How people get along with each other

Although personality is important for understanding yourself and others, your behaviour is influenced by something far more powerful: other people.

At least some of the time other people are a positive influence. We cooperate and get along with one another, and this has made us flourish as a species. Homo sapiens are remarkable for their ability to work together.

Having other people around improves our abilities

Even just the presence of others can help us. Research shows that having an audience can make you run or cycle faster and do simple tasks more quickly. The presence of others causes our bodies to go into a state of readiness, with increased heart rate, blood pressure and sensory alertness. The physiological arousal gives our performance a boost, this enhancement being known as 'social facilitation'.

But would we want an audience in every performance situation? Not necessarily, as the helpful effect only goes so far. An audience can hamper our performance on difficult or unfamiliar tasks. Physiological arousal and the fear of being judged interferes with our performance on harder tasks, such as answering questions about unfamiliar material, maths problems and learning difficult word lists.

So if you have to do some kind of test as part of a job application, if you get the choice it is probably best to do it alone if the test is difficult. But if you want to boost your performance in something you know well, then it is better to do it in company.

I'll scratch your back, you scratch mine

When someone does you a favour, do you feel the urge to give something in return? Most of us do. The urge to pay back – to reciprocate – is at the heart of our facility for cooperation. Our lives are built on giving something to others to get something back. Reciprocity works at all levels of society. Our personal relationships have a balance of give and take, while in the commercial world we are willing to pay a fair price for services or goods. Most of us are happy to give our employers a day's work in return for pay and we are willing to pay our taxes in return for good government.

> the urge to pay back – to reciprocate – is at the heart of our facility for cooperation

brilliant example

Our urge to reciprocate is powerful enough to override rational decision-making. What would make you more likely to fill in and post a survey – a reward of one dollar or fifty dollars? Researchers discovered that one dollar can be a stronger incentive. They sent out a survey with the promise of 50 dollars payment, and had a very low return rate. But when they sent people a one dollar note upfront, and a note of thanks, the return rate was significantly higher. Getting a dollar for nothing triggered a sense of obligation and the urge to pay the favour back.

The art of manipulation

Even a small gesture or gift can trigger the urge to reciprocate. Charities and businesses often send us small tokens such as a keyring or a pen, because they know it is a successful strategy in getting us to return the favour.

Another method for enhancing cooperation doesn't cost them anything. If a charity worker asked you to give up a day to take troubled youngsters to the zoo, would you agree? Eighty per cent of people say no. But researchers then asked another question first: they asked people to volunteer for two hours every week for two years. When people turned them down, the researchers agreed the request was unreasonable, and asked them to volunteer for the single day at the zoo instead. Using this method, 50 per cent of people said yes.

The reason this works is because people feel the questioner has done them a favour by backing down from the original request. So they feel obliged to reciprocate.

brilliant tip

If you want someone to say yes to a request, try asking them a big favour first, then agree it is unreasonable and ask for something smaller. If you would like your teenager to tidy her room, first of all ask her to tidy the house.

Use your awareness of this technique to resist manipulation from politicians, salesmen or unreasonable bosses – remember that by backing down from an unreasonable request they have not done you a favour at all. Being aware that it is a deliberate technique, deployed to manipulate your sense of reciprocity, can help you resist the urge to say yes.

Altruism: the human capacity to help others

Of course, we do not always expect payback from others when we do a good deed. Humans are capable of enormous feats of altruism, helping others at a cost to themselves with no expectation of reward.

brilliant example

Heroes of the 88th floor

On 9/11 when the plane crashed into the World Trade Center, Frank de Martini, an architect, and Pablo Ortiz, a construction inspector, were on the 88th floor, just below the impact zone. Instead of descending to safety, they went up.

On the 91st floor they cleared rubble and prised doors open, freeing trapped survivors and saving at least 70 people. When the tower collapsed, they both lost their lives.

What moves people to help others at such enormous cost? There appear to be basic mechanisms in social animals which make us want to help others. Brain research shows that giving to others activates parts of the brain involved with attachment and bonding. Altruistic behaviour depends on our ability to empathise with suffering and feel compassion for the victim. Researchers Oliner and Oliner interviewed people who helped rescue Jews from the Nazis and found that they had more empathy than similar people who did not help.

Psychologists used to be puzzled by altruism, as at first glance it goes against 'survival of the fittest' for an individual. However, a group of humans who were selfish all the time would leave fewer offspring than another group who provided kindness to families, friends, neighbours and strangers. Sometimes, it is a case of 'survival of the nicest'. On an individual level, as a social animal it can pay to be a good group member – if you are valued by the group

> sometimes, it is a case of 'survival of the nicest'

you will flourish and reduce your risk of being ostracised. Unselfishness gives us survival benefits in the long run.

In what situations are people more likely to show altruism? Psychology research confirms common sense: you are more likely to be helpful when you are in a good mood and to people who are physically attractive, or similar to you in looks, dress or attitudes. Research shows that even an insignificant similarity, such as having the same forename or date of birth makes people more inclined to be helpful.

People are more altruistic if they are feeling guilty about something. The guilt does not have to be anything to do with the situation in hand. Experimenters made a sample of people feel guilty by tricking them into thinking they had accidently broken a camera, and found that this induced guilt made them more likely to be helpful later.

brilliant tip

Want to encourage people to help you? Catch them in a good mood and look as attractive as you can. Aim to find genuine similarities between you and the other person – draw their attention to things you have in common, such as liking the same holiday destination, music or food. If possible, dress in a similar style to them – for example, if hoping for a loan from an uncle who likes to dress casually, don't dress smartly to impress but instead match his jeans and T-shirt.

So far, these findings fit in with our everyday experience. But here is something a bit more surprising: dwelling on your own death will make you more generous. Researchers asked people to write about what happens to their bodies after death. After contemplating their own mortality, people made bigger donations to charity. But they were only more generous to charities for people in their own countries.

dwelling on your own death will make you more generous

One explanation for this is called 'terror management theory'. Because we fear death, we have a coping strategy of holding onto our own culture, the shared set of values that gives our life meaning. So contemplating our own death makes us more generous to our own people but not those living in another culture.

When altruism fails: the bystander effect

A famous example in psychology is a 1960s murder in New York. A woman called Kitty Genovese was stalked and stabbed to death, and no one came to her aid or called the police despite the fact that there were 38 witnesses to the attack. This account is now thought to be exaggerated – there were fewer witnesses than claimed and some people did try to help – but the murder shocked the community and moved psychologists to try to understand why people did not help her more.

This led to the discovery of the 'bystander effect', one of the most reliable findings in social psychology. The more people there are around, the less likely we are to help someone out in an emergency. For example, one study showed that when female experimenters faked injury, shouting and crying out in pain, they could expect to be 'rescued' 70 per cent of the time if a nearby person was on their own. But if the bystander was in the company of just one other person, the 'rescue' rate dropped to 40 per cent.

Why is this? One reason is called 'diffusion of responsibility': everyone thinks someone else might take the responsibility of acting. Another explanation is that people are afraid of behaving in ways that are out of the norm. Finally, in situations where people are not sure what to do, they copy what other people are doing. In the bystander effect that is nothing, but the good side of this is that once one person has stopped to help, other people stop to help too.

brilliant insight

Now that you know about the bystander effect, you may be less prone to it. Research shows that people who have been educated about the bystander effect are more likely to be the first to step forward to help a person in distress.

What are morals and where do they come from?

Whether you actually help someone or not, most people would agree that it is the right thing to do. The vast majority of people have an intrinsic sense of morality. Morality is an important underpinning to our positive behaviour towards each other. We have rules about what is, and what is not, decent conduct and we try to abide by them.

For example, look at these behaviours – are they wrong, and if so, why?

- Cleaning a toilet with your country's flag
- Having sex with a dead chicken

Most people sense that these are wrong, but struggle to say exactly why. Why does our moral compass point that way? Is it just feeling or is there an inherent guiding force in our psychology? Is our moral compass the result of teaching or is it innate?

Psychologist Jonathan Haidt, who devised the above two examples, believes that to some extent morality is an innate instinct. He has discovered that people in different cultures have similar ideas about right and wrong. He believes that all human societies are based on the same six moral foundations.

The six moral foundations

1 Care/harm. Our basic instinct is to feel upset about the suffering of others and avoid harming them. This moral underlies altruism and our helpful, caring behaviour.

2 Fairness/cheating. Our sense of reciprocity is underpinned by this moral; it guides our beliefs about justice and personal rights.

3 Liberty/oppression. This is our feeling that we have a right to freedom of choice and to not be controlled or dominated by others.

4 Loyalty/betrayal. The moral we have about being true to our country, our family or social group.

5 Authority/subversion. When we show deference and respect to leaders or tradition, it is because of this moral foundation. The origin is our hierarchal nature: some members of our group are given more power or status than others.

6 Purity/sanctity. The moral based on our instinctive feeling of disgust about contamination. Contamination can be physical, or the more abstract, moral contamination.

According to Haidt, these moral foundations explain our feelings about the previous two examples. The reason sex with a dead chicken is wrong is because it offends our sense of purity/sanctity, as we feel both physical and moral disgust. Cleaning a toilet with your country's flag is wrong as it offends your sense of loyalty to your group.

People often falsely accuse each other of having no morals. Other people are usually just as moral as we are, but their sense is based on different foundations. For example, people who are happy to have casual sex emphasise their moral right to freedom of choice; those that believe it is wrong emphasise their sense of purity/sanctity.

brilliant insight

Many human conflicts are about different views of right and wrong. For example, your partner may believe they have a moral right to freedom and stay out late at night; you believe they should show loyalty by being with you. Next time you have an argument with someone, ask yourself, are you arguing because you have different moral foundations? If that is the case, you are unlikely to persuade them to see it your way, and you both probably need to compromise.

Want to discover your own moral foundations profile? Visit www.YourMorals.org

The dark side of morals

Morals are not always a force for good. It is our moral sense that drives us to commit acts of revenge and retribution, and moral outrage underlies our urge to punish others for their transgressions. For example, violent husbands often feel justified in hitting disobedient wives for refusing to recognise their authority. Psychologist Steven Pinker believes that it is moral outrage that motivates people to torture, murder and commit genocide. The dark side of morality will be covered in more depth in Chapter 6.

Friendship

Our sense of morality is important for effective cooperation, and so is friendship. Having friends is so important to us, it even seems to be good for our physical health. Socially isolated people are more likely to die early than people with a wider social network.

brilliant insight

Research reveals that friendlessness is as bad for your mortality as smoking 15 cigarettes a day, alcohol abuse or not taking any exercise. People who are lonely are twice as likely to die early as someone who is obese. Those who have frequent interactions with others in a social network have a 50 per cent better survival rate. Researchers conclude that doctors should pay as much attention to loneliness as any other health risk factor.

Why does friendship matter so much? It is partly because relationships influence our health behaviours – we are more likely to look after our health and see a doctor when needed. But in addition, friends help us cope with stress, and give meaning and purpose to our lives, which seems to have a health benefit of its own.

Do you feel you are discerning and selective in your choice of friends? Most people do, but it appears that friendship is more about chance. Peter Ustinov, the actor, once said 'I do not believe that friends are necessarily the people you like best, they are merely the people who got there first'.

Research has proved Ustinov right. Psychologists randomly allocated students to seats in a room at the beginning of term. One year later students were likely to be friends with the person they had happened to sit next to on the first day.

And if you think you select friends for their outstanding qualities, friends that challenge and stretch you, the truth is that you more likely select them because they are like you. People befriend others of a similar age, ethnic group, personality and attitude.

How do friendships develop? The way friendships become established is that we gradually reveal more about ourselves, and if the other person similarly self-discloses then the relationship develops. Too much or too little self-disclosure can make potential friendships founder. When a friendship is dissolving, people reduce the quality and intimacy of the information they reveal. So when you hear your friend's personal news through a third party, you know the relationship is in trouble.

Our sense of humour

Why do we spend so much time with each other and form friendships? One of the reasons is our sense of humour. Robin Dunbar believes humour evolved because it creates social bonds. Laughter causes a surge of endorphins, the 'feel-good' hormone. He says that instead of grooming each other physically, as apes do, to release endorphins, we make each other feel good by making each other laugh. Experimenters found that after strangers watched a comedy video and laughed together, they were just as generous to each other as if they knew each other very well.

> humour evolved because it creates social bonds

'Laughter turns strangers into friends.'

Robin Dunbar

Next time you are in a social situation, watch people interacting and listen to the comments that provoke laughter. How much of their humour would you say is genuinely witty?

Studies of humour show that most laughter is triggered by fairly mundane remarks, like 'Here we go again' or 'Not likely'. Plenty of remarks will have no inherent humour at all, but are said in a laughing tone and receive laughter in response. One expert, Robert Provine, says most human conversations are like 'an interminable situation comedy scripted by an extremely ungifted writer'. Laughing is often about social bonds, rather than wit.

Humour may also be a mechanism for coping with aggression and dominance. Instead of fighting, people 'laugh it off'. Humour is often about taking people down a peg or two. It is funny if your pompous, overbearing boss trips and falls flat on his face, but not if a frail, old lady does. This may explain why men generate more humour than women, as they are more likely to be involved in aggressive behaviour and conflicts over status.

As well as providing these vital social functions, laughter appears to support immune functioning and promote healing after illness.

Non-stop gossip

Another favourite social pastime is exchanging information about our own and other people's personal lives.

Psychologist Robin Dunbar eavesdropped on people talking in public places such as bars, trains and university canteens. He found that whatever the setting, about 65 per cent of casual human conversation is gossip. Men gossip just as much as women but their conversation tends to be about themselves and their own relationships, whereas women talk more about other people.

exchanging social information is vital for a smooth-running social life

Sharing news about who is doing what with whom comes so naturally to us that we do not even question why we are doing it. But why spend all this time on gossip? According to Dunbar, exchanging social information is vital for a smooth-running social life. We have to remember who is a rival, a cheat, a friend, an ally, who gets on with whom and who are lovers or enemies. Keeping track of who is doing what and why helps us predict behaviour and make better social decisions. We are hungry to hear news about the powerful, high status individuals in our lives, as their behaviour probably has more important implications for our own survival.

Today many of us gossip about a celebrity, leader or figure who we will never meet – our minds mistake the people we see in magazines, newspapers and on television for important members of our 'tribe'. Headlines are about love matches, sexual behaviour, infidelity, rivals, conflicts, status, physical appearance, health, illness – all issues relevant to survival and reproduction.

brilliant action

Next time you can overhear someone's casual conversation, for example on the bus or in a coffee shop, try to figure out how much of the conversation in gossip. Is it between 60 and 70 per cent?

Our intertwining social networks

We are connected to each other through our relationships not just with our friends, but relatives, co-workers and neighbours. And through them, we are connected to all their friends, relatives, co-workers and neighbours, and so on. These social networks have a powerful effect on our behaviour, influencing our beliefs, feelings and even our physical and mental health. Scientists Nicholas Christakis and James Fowler say that research on social networks reveals that obesity, smoking, depression and even happiness can spread through the population like a contagion.

If you have a friend who puts on weight, you are three times as likely to put on weight too. And if your friend has a friend who has put on weight, this too will increase your chances of weight gain. You don't have to meet someone to be affected by them – studies suggest there is an effect at three degrees of separation, implying that if your friend's friend's friend over-eats then this will put you at risk of weight gain, too. Your friend's neighbour's workmate can make you fat.

Why does this happen? You copy what you see or hear other people doing. For example, we are more likely to donate blood if we see someone else agreeing to give blood first. Ideas about how to behave spread from person to person. If your friend has lots of friends who are fat, we feel this is normal and unconsciously follow suit. As writer Eric Hoffer put it: 'When people are free to do as they please, they usually imitate each other.'

brilliant insight

Your behaviour affects not just the people you come in contact with, but the people they know, and the people they know. So if you are kind to people, take up exercise and give up smoking, people you never meet will feel the influence of this and be kinder, give up smoking and take exercise, too.

Living in status hierarchies

In all human societies there is a concept of social status, with the higher in status having more access to resources. Instead of having endless fights we agree to a hierarchy where the lower ranking person submits to the higher ranking one. Thus many physical fights are avoided.

We might think that hierarchies and deference to our betters belongs to a bygone age, no longer so important in our liberal, modern society. Yet status is alive and well, in a multitude of more complex forms than doffing one's cap to the local squire.

Study hierarchies at your work place. If you bump into your boss in a doorway, you will likely let him or her go first, and when talking you will let them guide the conversation to topics they choose. Each subgroup has its own metrics for ranking one another: for academics it might be number of papers published, for actors it might be looks, for bankers the size of their annual bonus. Some people consider the make and model of their car to be crucial in placing them in a social ranking. Others might laugh at this display, yet be just as keen to publicise their own status in how much charity money they have raised. For one group of people ranking can be signalled via fashionable hand-bags, for others via the productivity of an allotment.

How do you perceive your own status within your own various social groups? In one social arena, such as the workplace, you might see yourself as being low ranking and behave more sub-missively, while in your family arena you might see yourself as top ranking and behave quite differently.

Have a think about your own behaviour and motivations. How much of what you do or buy is driven by a desire to express your status, to define yourself amid the various rankings and hierarchies of your life?

How to spot dominance and hierarchies

How can you tell who are the dominant individuals?

The quantity of speech is a key way to assess this – dominant people talk more. They also try to influence others more often. Something you might observe in the workplace is that when a lower ranking person speaks, they address the person at the top, whereas when the top rank person speaks it is to the whole group. Eye contact is another indication: assess people on whether they have 'hard' or 'soft' eye contact. Other body lan-guage gives clues: look for people who stand up straight, do not smile much and talk in a loud voice. It will come as no surprise that people who are physically attractive, well-groomed, athletic, intelligent and humorous are more likely to be dominant. Research shows that dominant individuals are also better at lying.

The continual creation of hierarchies

In 1970, Fisek and Ofshe put groups of people together and assessed dominance by quantity of speech. They found that within one minute, half of the group had formed a hierarchy. In the next five minutes the rest did.

Wherever we go and wherever groupings form, humans will tend to form dominance hierarchies. The potential for conflict is greatly reduced: there is unspoken agreement that where there is a conflict of interest, the higher status individuals will win out. Instead of coming to blows, one person sizes another up and submits via body language, for example, with lowered eyes, a less erect body posture and dipped head. The acceptance of their place in a status hierarchy makes it easy for two people to be together, an agreement to co-exist without conflict so long as each knows their place.

The danger of losing status

With loss of status comes negative emotions: shame, low mood and humiliation. Stories of a 'fall from grace' are a staple of literature. Politicians who lose an election describe how their rejection and loss of status were devastating to their lives.

our self-esteem is partly gauged by our standing in a social group

When people are made redundant or lose their jobs the loss of status can be as painful as the economic loss. Our self-esteem is partly gauged by our standing in a social group. This is called sociometer theory. The respect given to us by other people gives us an indication of how valued we are, and this becomes part of our self-image. A loss of status often brings a loss of self-esteem.

The human need to belong

People like to feel they belong in a group. People identify themselves with a group on the flimsiest basis.

On a whim, Danny Wallace put an advert in a magazine saying 'Join me' and asked people to send in a passport-sized photo of themselves. Despite the fact that he did not give any reason to join him, he was inundated with photos. He eventually decided that his group would have a purpose – carrying out random acts of kindness on a Friday.

The need to belong and the fear of being rejected has its roots in our evolutionary past. Being ejected from the group would have meant almost certain death.

People are quick to classify each other as belonging or not belonging to our group. If we judge someone as 'in-group', we see them in a favourable light and are likely to cooperate with them. When we assign someone to the category 'others', we are likely to discriminate against them.

The desire to conform

We have a strong instinct to conform with a group. In a classic psychological study, Solomon Asch asked groups of people to look at a printed line on a piece of card and pick out a line of the same length on another piece of card. It was an easy task – the other lines to choose from were obviously too long or too short – however, except for the one individual being tested, everyone else in the group was a stooge instructed to call out the wrong answer.

What would you do in this situation, faced with others in your group calling out what you think is an obviously wrong answer?

Stand out alone or conform? In the experiment, 75 per cent of people called out the wrong answer at least once, rather than go against the majority view. People would rather go against their own opinions than risk ridicule and disapproval for going against group norms. This is called 'normative social influence'.

The people in Asch's experiment showed much more courage in voicing their opinion if just one other person disagreed first. Even if someone called out an alternative wrong answer it gave people courage to be a dissenting voice, too. The practical application of this is: speak out, even if you are afraid you will be the lone voice in a group – there is a good chance others will join you.

Study after study has shown that we tend to conform to whatever we feel is normal for our particular group. Teenagers are particularly affected by normative social influence. As teenagers, we may see ourselves as rebellious but really we are often just conforming to our peer group. A rebellious tattoo, intended as an expression of individuality, is often a just a mark of belonging to a group.

brilliant tip

If you want to influence others, use the power of norms. You can do this by stating that the majority of the group are doing the thing you want. For example, if you would like your workmates to keep the coffee area tidy, say something like: 'Everyone in this office clears up after themselves, there's only a few who do not.' Research shows that the alternative, 'Everyone in this office leaves this place in a mess, I wish people would clear up', will make the behaviour worse – hearing that everyone else is messy makes people feel it is normal.

The trouble with conformity

The instinct we have to conform causes problems. When we are together, people start agreeing more and more with each other as the discussion progresses, and the group position becomes exaggerated towards one side or another. Groups make more extreme decisions than individuals, and this is known as 'polarisation'.

For example, studies of mock juries show that when individual members of a jury feel lenient towards a defendant, they will make an even more lenient decision when they have deliberated over the judgement together. On the other hand, if the individual jury members want to dole out a fairly harsh punishment, they will hand out an even more extreme punishment after discussing it as a group.

How can you influence a whole group if you disagree with the majority? Studies show that if you persist in voicing a minority view, you can sway the whole group. However, you need to be consistent in voicing your view – if you waver, you will not influence them. A dissenting voice is often good for group decision-making. When a minority view is expressed, the group considers more options and engages in more elaborate, considered thinking.

Profile: Kurt Lewin

Kurt Lewin (1890–1947) was the first psychologist to point to the importance of the *situation* in determining our behaviour, in particular the immediate social situation. He is seen as the 'father' of social psychology.

Lewin was born and brought up in Germany and fought in the First World War, receiving the Iron Cross for bravery. In 1933, he moved to America because of Hitler's persecution of the Jews. His experiences in Nazi Germany shaped his view of the importance of social forces and he was the first psychologist to study these scientifically.

Some of his most well-known research was on the social effects of an 'authoritarian' leadership style. He studied groups of children and found that immediately after the introduction of an authoritarian

▶

leader, children become apathetic, demotivated and low in energy, whereas previously they had been lively, cheerful and creative. Before Lewin, psychologists had seen behaviour as being a product of an individual's past and neglected the importance of the immediate situation.

Kurt Lewin died of a heart attack aged 56, after writing eight psychology books and more than 80 articles. Although not a household name, many regard Lewin as one of the most important psychologists of the twentieth century.

Groupthink

When groups have high levels of cohesiveness, it not only produces extreme decisions, but can produce flawed ones, particularly in high-stress situations. This is the phenomenon known as groupthink. Where groups are highly cohesive and under pressure, they can become blinkered, closed-minded and focus far more on reaching agreement than on the reality or morals of the situation.

An illustration is the Challenger shuttle disaster in 1986, when seven astronauts lost their lives after the space shuttle exploded seconds after take-off. Some individual engineers had misgivings about the safety of launching after a night of freezing temperatures, but when they came together in a group they conformed to the group pressure not to disrupt the launch plans.

According to psychologist Irving Janis, there are some techniques for preventing groupthink:

- Powerful members of the group should hold their opinions back until others have aired theirs.
- All members of the group should be encouraged to express criticism and doubts.

- One person should have the role of devil's advocate.
- Outside opinion should be invited.
- Ensure alternative options are considered.
- Get independent groups working on the same problem.

Our urge to cooperate has a dark side, and although we have a great capacity for cooperation, there is another side to human life: conflict. We are not a race of peaceful cooperators – we cheat, we lie and we fight. This is the subject of Chapter 6.

brilliant recap

- Understanding people is not just about looking at the individual; we need to consider social influences.
- Many of our everyday experiences - humour, laughter, friendship, gossip - are mechanisms for ensuring social cohesion.
- Much of our behaviour is determined by the pressure to cooperate with others.
- We are influenced and governed by moral pressures, hierarchical status and group dynamics.
- Group and social influences can override our individual wishes, eliciting cruel behaviour from a normally kind person, and making clever people do stupid things.

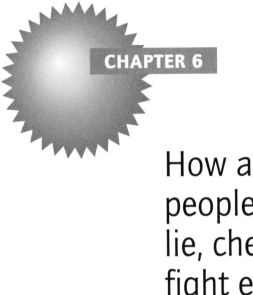

CHAPTER 6

How and why
people betray,
lie, cheat and
fight each
other

art of our psychology is geared to cooperation. We help each other and have a great capacity for harmony. But we are also in competition with each other, so another way of benefiting from living in social groups is to use other human beings for our own ends. There are many situations in life where it pays more to exploit others than to cooperate. So some of our psychology is also centred on dealing with conflict.

There is a tension in life: should we be peacefully cooperative and resist the benefits of using others just for our own gain? Or should we get ahead by cheating and exploiting people? This tension is at the heart of being a social animal. Life is often about negotiating a way through these dilemmas.

It is dangerous to trust people all the time

Imagine two people who have committed a crime together. They have both been arrested and held in separate cells. But the evidence against them is flimsy, and there will only be a conviction if one of them testifies against the other. They have these options:

- If they both keep quiet, they will each be sentenced to only one month in prison.
- If only one person testifies against the other, he will go free and the other man will get a one-year sentence.
- If they both testify against each other, they will both get six months in prison.

What would you do? This is the famous Prisoner's Dilemma, an illustration of the tension between cooperation and conflict, and is one of many examples in 'game theory'. Game theory is used by psychologists as a way to analyse decision-making. Many situations in life can be modelled as 'games' with rules, goals and strategies. Studying the way people make decisions in these games can be used to predict how people will behave.

In the Prisoner's Dilemma, most people take the safest option: testify against their partner. If you think your partner will talk, then it is best if you talk as well, getting six months in jail instead of a year. If you think your partner will stay silent, it's still better to testify, going free instead of having a month in prison.

Rational action for each individual is to betray and cheat on the other. Yet the best option for the two combined would be if they cooperated and remain silent – so long as they could completely trust each other.

If we are totally trusting we risk exploitation by those who lie, cheat, steal, betray or inflict harm on us. So rather than taking this risk, we take action against others first. The tragedy is that human beings often feel compelled to harm others becase of the fear of being harmed themselves.

When did you last tell a lie?

Most people tell at least one lie every day. Much of the time, these lies have good intent and act as a 'social lubricant'. The vast majority of people lie in the interests of harmonious relationships. You tell your friends they do not look fat when they do, you tell relatives you love the gift that you actually gave to the charity shop.

Apart from white lies, everyone cares about honesty. In opinion polls honesty is usually cited as one of the top five characteristics that people look for in their friends, lovers or leaders.

But is this wishful thinking? People lie and deceive because it works – deception can give an advantage and is probably an inherent part of human nature. Deception is common even in the animal kingdom.

brilliant example

Dishonest frogs

Green frogs croak loudly to ward off rivals, and the bigger the frog, the deeper the croak. This deep sound is more threatening to others. So small frogs use deception: they lower their voices so they can produce a more impressive-sounding croak.

With our superior intellect, imagination and language abilities, we humans turn deception into a fine art.

Psychologist Paul Ekman has conducted extensive research on lying and says the most common motive for lying is to avoid being punished for a misdeed. The second most common motive is to get a reward that cannot be won through honest means. Other motives are:

- to protect someone else
- to prevent risk of physical harm, such as deceiving a would-be attacker by saying you have already called the police
- to get admiration from others
- to escape from an awkward social situation, for example, saying you are busy to avoid going to a boring party
- to avoid embarrassment
- to maintain privacy
- to exercise power over others by withholding information.

Can you spot a liar?

While many people are confident that they are good at detecting lies, the reality is that most people are not. In studies of lie detection, most people do little better than chance. Even professionals like judges, police officers and forensic psychiatrists often do no better. Skilled liars can fool anyone. A famous example is when Hitler lied to the British Prime Minister, Neville Chamberlain, convincing him he had no hostile intent. Chamberlain wrote in a letter at the time: 'I got the impression that here was a man who could be relied upon when he had given his word.'

skilled liars can fool anyone

There is no single clue in behaviour or speech that is a unique sign of dishonesty. Many people have the idea that certain signs, such as avoiding eye contact, are evidence of lying but this is not true. Some people look deliberately into people's eyes when lying in an attempt to appear more truthful because they know people believe this myth. Signs such as 'shifty eyes' or someone squirming in their seat can be misleading – they might be revealing a fear of being thought dishonest, rather than fear of being caught in a lie.

Paul Ekman has discovered some behavioural clues that, when taken together, can be used to spot a liar. Using these methods, he found he could distinguish truth from lies about 80 to 90 per cent of the time. Some signs of lying are as follows:

A leaky facial expression

When people are lying, they sometimes need to conceal an emotion. Most people find it difficult to completely suppress emotions and they 'leak' through in facial expression or behaviour. Ekman calls this 'emotional leakage'. Emotions can betray themselves through 'micro expressions'. Some emotions have a characteristic facial expression, and this fleetingly appears on the person's face, for just a fraction of a second. They are difficult to spot; most people do not notice them without special training.

Ekman discovered micro expressions when he studied the video-tape of a depressed woman in a psychiatric hospital, who had lied about feeling better because she wanted to be released in order to kill herself. After studying the tape for hours, he noticed that at one point she showed a fleeting expression of despair, which she quickly covered up with a smile.

Frequent contradictions

To lie you need a good memory, and although people who tell the truth sometimes contradict themselves, liars do it more often.

Reduced hand movements

When talking naturally, most people unconsciously use their hands to illustrate their speech – Ekman calls these 'illustra-tors', but these tend to reduce or stop altogether when someone is lying. As in all behavioural cues, this does not necessarily indicate lying; illustrators also decrease with boredom.

Distancing language

This is when a person talks in a way that puts themselves at an emotional distance from the subject. They might reduce the amount of times they say 'I' and use words that reduce the impact of the behaviour, for example, when denying infidelity they don't say the direct 'I did not have sex' they say something like 'there was nothing too friendly going on'.

Fake emotions

Liars sometimes have cause to 'put on' emotions they do not feel. Faked emotions may start and stop too abruptly, or come on in the wrong place. Also, some parts of facial expression are difficult or impossible to fake. A genuine smile involves muscles around the eyes and raises the cheeks, known as the 'Duchenne' smile. A fake smile uses muscles around the mouth only.

In genuine sadness or distress, the forehead muscles are involved – the inner corners of the eyebrows are pulled upward, producing characteristic wrinkles. Similarly, in fear, the eyebrows are raised and pulled together, and the forehead wrinkles, which is also hard to fake.

Thinking too much

A possible sign of lying is too many pauses or errors in speech, indicating that the person is concentrating on working out the answer when the answer should not require much thinking. Lying takes more cognitive effort than truth-telling.

brilliant action

How to improve your ability to detect lies

- Get the person relaxed and off-guard. Do not show suspicion or throw accusations at people, as this makes them close up. An ordinary conversational style aimed at just getting information is better. The more the other person speaks, the more opportunities there are for them to show a clue they may be lying.

- Don't pay attention to one particular aspect of their behaviour – you need to look for multiple signs. People who are better at lie detection do not rely on one sign, they look at a range of information.

- Get to know a person's unique style – sometimes people have their own individual profile of clues that they are lying.

- Ask for details of their story, then talk about unrelated topics for a while, then go back to the details with different questions. It can be hard for a liar to remember the information they have given, leading to inconsistencies about minor points.

- Pay close attention when the person is giving their story for the first time. You are more likely to be successful at detecting a lie when they have not told it before. As in any other behaviour, a chance to practise improves the liar's performance.

But Ekman emphasises it is not possible to be confident about spotting liars in everyday life. To reach his level of accuracy of 80 to 90 per cent requires many hours of going over tapes.

Cheating: a key part of human nature

One of the aims of deception is to try to get an advantage over others as in cheating, swindling or stealing. Cheating and stealing violate our principle of social exchange. Human society is governed by a wide variety of social contracts, the conventions that we are expected to abide by, some of which are enshrined in law and some of which are simply seen as correct behaviour. But we are vulnerable to 'free-riders', people who do not pay the usual price for a benefit.

Some psychologists, such as Leda Cosmides and John Tooby, argue that our minds are wired to be good at spotting these cheats. Try the following demonstration – see if you can solve these two puzzles:

Puzzle 1:

You have four cards, each with a letter on one side of the card and a number on the back. Here are the four cards:

The rule is: if a card has a D rating, then it must be marked code 3 on the back. Which card or cards should you turn over to find out if this is rule is being broken?

Puzzle 2:

You say to four friends that they can borrow your car while you are away. But you have a rule that if they borrow your car, they should pay for the petrol.

When you get back, your four friends each write down what they did on a card. On one side of the card they write whether they borrowed your car, on the other side whether they have paid for petrol. Here are the four cards:

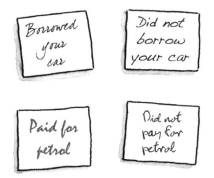

Which card or cards do you need to turn over to find out if one of your friends has cheated you out of petrol money?

You need to turn over the first and last card for both puzzles. You need to turn 'Borrowed your car', hoping to see 'Paid for petrol' on the other side. And you need to turn over 'Did not pay for petrol', to find out if this person borrowed your car. About 75 per cent of people get this right. But very few people are able to solve the first puzzle.

Logically, puzzle 1 is identical to puzzle 2. You are just finding out whether an 'if-then' is being broken. For puzzle 1 you needed to turn over D and 7 to find out if the rule is being violated – it is exactly the same conceptually.

When the puzzle is presented as a social exchange you can solve it more easily; when presented as abstract logic you struggle. Cosmides and Tooby believe this is because our minds are wired to spot cheaters.

Our cognitive abilities seem to get a boost when it comes to dealing with double-crossers. For example, what is your memory like for faces? Researchers showed people some photographs of faces and said that some of the characters in the photos had cheated someone out of a sum of money. People were much better at remembering the faces of the 'cheats'.

What makes people cheats?

Psychological studies of con artists show that the majority see themselves as justified in their actions.

People who swindle others believe they are 'owed', for example that they were treated unfairly so they have a moral right to the goods. In other words, they have a distorted sense of reciprocity. Another reason is that cheats usually start off small, and then become bolder. Small steps on the road to dishonesty lead to bigger ones. And, as always, when people see other people doing something they follow suit. So cheaters often say that 'other people were doing it'.

> small steps on the road to dishonesty lead to bigger ones

A real-life swindler

Joyti De-Laurey cheated by portraying herself as a trustworthy PA while using her position to steal over £4 million from her bosses at the investment bank Goldman Sachs. She started by forging a cheque to herself for £4,000 and became bolder, eventually taking £2 million in one go. She enjoyed a lavish lifestyle, buying Cartier jewellery, a villa in Cyprus, luxury cars and a house for a friend. According to media reports she felt that, as she worked hard for her bosses, she

▶

deserved more, especially when she saw how those super-rich bosses at Goldman Sachs lived. She said they would spend half a million on a birthday party. Joyti felt that her employers owed her. Her diary at the time said 'I need one more helping of what's mine'.

She was eventually caught and sentenced to seven years in prison. She was released after three and a half and now works at a charity for offenders.

Aggression

The most brutal way to get an advantage over others is to use physical aggression. Aggression is defined as 'behaviour with the intent to cause harm to others who do not want to be harmed'.

Psychologists distinguish between 'emotional aggression', fuelled by 'hot' feelings such as anger and hatred, and 'instrumental aggression', harmful acts which are performed in a calculated way. An example of instrumental aggression is where the criminal coolly shoots a security guard dead in order to get into a building, as a 'means to an end'.

The majority of instrumental aggression is not carried out by criminal psychopaths, but by ordinary people with a normal capacity of empathy. What makes ordinary people carry out monstrous acts? Here are two reasons: obedience and ideology.

1 Obedience

Psychologist Stanley Milgram wanted to understand why so many people in Nazi Germany committed atrocities against the Jews in the Second World War. The majority of these people were not psychopaths, but colluded in exterminating men, women and children. Their justification was that they were only following orders. But will an ordinary person commit violence just because they are told to do so? To answer this question Milgram conducted his now famous series of experiments on obedience to authority.

Milgram asked people to give electric shocks to a 'learner' strapped to a chair in a separate cubicle. People were told to shock the learner if they made an error, and to increase the level of shock, from 'mild' through to 'danger, severe shock' right up to a maximum of 450 volts.

The learner was a confederate and the electric shocks were fake. The 'learner' acted in a more and more distressed way as the shocks increased, portraying their part convincingly by groaning, shouting, kicking the wall and begging to be released from the experiment. At 450 volts the 'learner' fell silent, apparently either unconscious or dead.

How many people were willing to go along with this apparently brutal and dangerous experiment? In a survey before the experiment, only 1 per cent of people said that they could see themselves agreeing to hurt someone in this way. But Milgram discovered that 65 per cent of people, both men and women, obeyed instructions to inflict the maximum 450 volts.

This was not because people enjoyed or wanted to inflict pain. The majority of people were distressed and reluctant to carry out the orders. But when they said they wanted to stop giving shocks, the experimenters prodded them with a series of escalating commands:

- Please continue.
- The experiment requires that you continue.
- It is absolutely essential that you continue.
- You have no other choice, you must go on.

Why did 65 per cent of people obey these orders? One reason is that it is a social norm to obey authority, and this has a powerful influence on our behaviour. Another process is 'gradualism': people started off with small electric shocks and each step was just a relatively small one.

Also, we do not feel responsible for our behaviour if someone else tells us to do it – we feel we are not personally accountable for our actions. These mundane forces can induce us to commit 'instrumental violence'.

'Ordinary people, doing ordinary jobs, and without any particular hostility on their part, can become agents in a terrible destructive process.'

Stanley Milgram

> our mundane and everyday inclination to cooperate and obey can bring hideous results

Milgram's notorious experiment shows that atrocities like the Holocaust are not caused by the intrinsic evil of a nation of people. Instead, our mundane and everyday inclination to cooperate and obey can bring hideous results. This has been dubbed as the 'banality of evil' by theorist Hannah Erendt.

Profile: Stanley Milgram

When he carried out his famous obedience experiments at Yale University, Stanley Milgram (1933–1984) was just 28, a recent PhD graduate from Harvard. Although these experiments were only one element of his research, they were to dominate his career. His ethics were challenged because of the stress he inflicted on participants, and many at the time were unwilling to accept his results and said his methodology was flawed. But further 'obedience to authority' investigations obtained the same findings again and again. Even today, similar studies, modified to be more ethical, show similar levels of obedience, even though culturally we have less respect for authority than back in 1961.

Milgram maintained that people objected to his obedience experiments because they showed an unwelcome truth about human nature. His findings changed our view of ourselves, proving that it does not make sense to 'demonise' another nation or group, because any of us are capable of committing unacceptable acts depending on the circumstances. Milgram believed that obedience to authority was part of our make-up, necessary for organising ourselves as a social species.

His findings brought home the key tenet of social psychology – our individual inclinations do not necessarily determine our behaviour. As he put it: 'The social psychology of this century reveals a major lesson: often it is not so much the kind of person a man is as the kind of situation in which he finds himself that determines how he will act.'

The controversy Milgram attracted meant he was never offered a full professorship at Harvard. He moved to the City University of New York where he was a popular teacher, experimenter and mentor, heading its psychology programme until his death of a heart attack aged just 51.

2 Ideology

Another factor probably played a part in the behaviour of participants in the Milgram study. They believed they were doing the 'right' thing. They believed that they were taking part in something for the greater good, a legitimate enterprise in the name of science. One of the reasons normal people can commit this type of violence is because of ideology. Psychologist Roy Baumeister points out that people are often willing to inflict harm for the greater good. We reason that the 'ends justify the means'. When people are in the grip of a belief system that involves the idea that harm needs to be inflicted for a greater ultimate benefit, then this is the green light for all sorts of violent behaviour. This ranges from hitting a child on the grounds that 'I'm doing this for your own good', up to the extermination of a group of people. Many Germans were persuaded to believe that killing Jews would ultimately create a peaceful utopia.

Emotional aggression

Of course, much violence springs from emotional motives, and the distinction between emotional and instrumental violence is outdated. In reality, the two motives often combine. For example, the parent who hits a child not only believes that they are doing the right thing, they are feeling angry, too. Hitler was motivated by hatred as well as ideology.

Angry aggression

Some aggression is fuelled by simple anger. Psychological findings on this support what common sense would tell us – aggression is more likely if someone is unexpectedly and unfairly frustrated, if hot, if drunk, if in a bad mood, if people see themselves as deprived and disadvantaged, or if confined in a small space and overcrowded.

But other common-sense understandings of aggression are not so accurate. Many people see aggression as a build-up of energy that needs an outlet. People say they need to 'release' their aggression and then they will calm down or achieve 'catharsis'. This misconception is based on Freud's idea that aggression is a basic drive, like hunger or thirst, that has to be sated rather than blocked. But research shows that people who are given the chance to express or act out their anger get more angry, not less. In one study, angry people were given the opportunity to give an electric shock to the person who had annoyed them. This did not make the angry individuals calm down. It had the opposite effect: they became more aggressive and punished their target even more.

brilliant tip

If you have to deal with an aggressive person, beware of encouraging them to 'vent' their feelings or punch bean bags. This will not dissipate their feelings of anger, and it may even make them worse.

Another common-sense understanding is that people are aggressive because they have low self-esteem. But research by Roy Baumeister shows this is not true. People with low self-esteem are less aggressive, and if anything it is the people who have inflated self-esteem who are more hostile. Baumeister found that when insulted, narcissistic people are more likely to be antagonistic – challenges to their grandiose views of themselves trigger aggressive responses. If you have to challenge a person with a big ego, do it in a way that helps them preserve their sense of self-esteem, otherwise expect retaliation.

Escalation of aggression

One of the main causes of aggression is: aggression. Sometimes just the fear that someone else is going to be aggressive will make people strike first. When verbally or physically threatened, a natural response is to be antagonistic back. Aggression therefore can quickly escalate: if one person shows a hostile verbal or non-verbal behaviour, the other retaliates in kind, quickly leading to a fight.

So if you are confronted by an aggressive person it is theoretically possible to reduce the chances of an argument escalating into an attack by deliberately resisting the instinct to behave aggressively back. There is little research on whether this de-escalation approach definitely works. When confronted by an aggressive person who you feel may be violent, then the best thing to do may be to get away safely if you can.

brilliant dos and don'ts

Dealing with an aggressive person

Do

✔ Give them plenty of personal space.

✔ Stand in a non-threatening body position, sideways on from them at around 90 degrees.

✔ Use respectful eye contact and look away frequently.

✔ Keep a non-threatening facial expression.

✔ Keep your arms by your sides or use submissive gestures such as holding your hands palms up.

✔ Apologise, even if you are not at fault – find something about the situation you can say you are sorry about.

✔ Agree with something in what they are saying.

✔ Use active listening: pay attention to them, show you are listening, for example, by saying things like 'I can see your point', or paraphrase their words to convey your understanding.

Don't

✗ Stand face to face, as this looks more aggressive.

✗ Step into their personal space.

✗ Use a threatening direct gaze or try to 'stare them down'.

✗ Put your hands on your hips, or use other hostile gestures such as finger pointing.

✗ Show hostility or contempt in your facial expression, such as eye rolls or sneering.

✗ Pass comment or pass judgement.

✗ Tell them what to do.

✗ Threaten, argue or challenge them.

✗ Do anything which looks as if you are trying to shame or disrespect them.

Fights over dominance

In practice, it is extremely difficult to resist the urge to respond to aggression with aggression. One of the reasons is that behaving submissively reduces our own sense of status. We think: 'I'm not taking this!' We feel ashamed and diminished if we back down when faced with threatening behaviour. Some people would rather risk losing their lives in a fight than risk losing 'face' this way.

The reason is to do with the human tendency to form dominance hierarchies. To a large extent, dominance hierarchies reduce aggression – instead of having endless fights, we size each other up and the less dominant person 'shows respect' and gives way to the more dominant person (as discussed in Chapter 5). This system does not prevent all aggression. People fight to retain their position in the pecking order or to try and rise in it. As psychologists Martin Daly and Margo Wilson point out, much violence is about losing or gaining social rank.

In much of modern life, this primitive system has been taken over by law and order. It no longer pays to assault someone, and social rank is measured in many ways other than ability to engage in violence. But in some cultures where the rule of law and order is not strong, this kind of physically aggressive dominance hierarchy still prevails. Statistics show this is mostly among 15- to 32-year-old men in deprived housing estates and in gangs. Many murders are the result of a fight over dominance, disproportionately carried out by young males with low social status.

Men who are concerned about their position in the hierarchy are sensitive to threats. Eye contact is one of the ways that respect or threat is signalled: direct gaze is disrespectful, lowered eyes shows respect. So a fight can break out from the most trivial beginning, a man believing himself to be the recipient of an insolent stare. This is seen as a failure to treat him according to his rightful place in the social hierarchy. If he retaliates with an aggressive comment, violence can quickly escalate.

 insight

Self-serving bias

After a fight, each person will be convinced they were in the right. They will both protest that they were just acting in self-defence, or were justified in their actions.

People's explanations of their own and others' behaviour are subject to bias. People view another person's behaviour as being caused by their internal attributes: for example, 'he hit me, because he is evil and malicious'. But they think that their own behaviour was caused by the situation: 'I hit him because the situation meant I had no choice.' This psychological bias is called the 'fundamental attribution error'.

Our desire for revenge

As Daly and Wilson point out, another motivation for aggressive behaviour is revenge. Twenty per cent of murders are estimated to be due to revenge, and it is a particularly common motive in school shootings, estimated at over 60 per cent. The need for revenge also moves people to enlist in terrorist organisations. Even people who show no violent behaviour entertain thoughts of revenge. A study of university students found that this was a common aggressive fantasy.

> revenge is the flip side of reciprocity

Revenge is the flip side of reciprocity. If someone has harmed us, we want to harm them back. This can lead to an endless cycle of 'payback' through the generations.

Although revenge causes much harm, it can also prevent violence as it serves as a deterrent. We do not harm people because we know they will get us back. An experiment on revenge showed people resisted the temptation to punish someone with an electric shock when they knew that person had the option to shock them back.

Trying to understand hatred

Not all aggressive acts can be explained by expediency, anger or revenge. Some violence is fuelled by the more complex emotion we know as the feeling of 'hatred'. For example, those who hate homosexuality may deliberately seek out gay people in order to commit violence against them. These are so-called 'hate crimes'. Hatred can be directed to an individual, group, nation or race. Hatred for the enemy is fostered by each side in a war.

Although hatred is an important and destructive force, it has not been studied as much as it warrants. Robert Sternberg proposes that hate is composed of a triangle of emotions:

1 Repulsion and disgust: Instead of seeking closeness to the hated person, you want distance – you are repelled by them. They have disgusting characteristics or behaviours. You see the object of your hate as subhuman or animal-like. This is the 'negation of intimacy' component.

2 Anger/fear: You experience autonomic arousal because of the hated person – intense anger or fear, or both. In other words, they trigger your fight or flight response, they evoke negative passions in you. This is the 'hot' aspect of hate; Sternberg terms it the 'passion' component.

3 Contempt: This component of hate is the devaluation of the hated person, who is seen as having no human worth or as subhuman. This is the 'decision-commitment' component.

Sternberg proposes that people experience different types of hate depending on how much of the three are experienced, for example:

- Cool hate: The hater feels mostly disgust towards their hated object; they are repelled by them and want nothing to do with them.

- Hot hate: The hater feels mostly anger or fear because of a threat – they are likely to be aggressive. An example of this is road rage.

- Burning hate: When people feel all three components, they are disgusted, infuriated and frightened by the hated person and see them as having no human worth. When people feel 'burning hate' they have a desire to eradicate the hated object.

Sternberg says that a person feeling one component of hate is a mild threat, people who feel two are a moderate threat and those who experience all three are a severe danger to others.

It is not really understood why some people feel hate more than others. Some studies of people who commit 'hate crimes' have found they are more likely when people have been brought up with aggression and have not had their basic needs met. Unsurprisingly, one of the causes of hate is being a victim of oppression – typically victims of prejudice hate their oppressors. Hate breeds hate: if you are a victim of hate you will hate them back.

> our morals can be a force for good but they have a dark side

Steven Pinker explains that another source of violent emotions may come from our human moral sensibilities. Our morals can be a force for good but they have a dark side. Morals can act as brakes on violent urges, but they can also be a green light – when people feel morals have been violated, then wrongdoers deserve punishment. For example, if you believe homosexuality is morally wrong, you may also believe that gay people have committed an offence and deserve punishment. Outraged morality can fuel hate and violent urges, for example, it is outraged morality that is behind so-called 'honour' killings of women seen to be 'unchaste'.

Hate is fuelled in situations where individuals or groups are seen as morally deficient, exploitative or undeservingly well-off. If one group of people has an ideology that elevates some, yet devalues others into a category of being different, stupid, lazy, impure or standing in the way of 'a better world', then the conditions for violence are created.

Groups of humans are dangerous

The above motives for violence can happen at an individual or group level, but it is people cooperating together to harm another group that causes the most large-scale destruction. The way people behave in groups makes this more likely to happen.

Even a minimal distinction between people can set up a group identity that is enough to make them want to harm the 'out-group'. Psychologist Henri Tajfel conducted an experiment where he told people they were in one of two groups – those who preferred the paintings of either Klee or Kandinsky. He then asked them to allocate money or fine people – people immediately preferred to give money to their own group members and to penalise the other group. Some psychologists believe that the very act of identifying with an in-group means derogation of the out-group. We automatically have less empathy for out-groups and are likely to believe, in the words of Krebs and Denton, that 'they are inferior: they are all alike: they will exploit us'.

In another notorious study, psychologist Muzafer Sherif divided boys on summer camp at Robbers Cave in California into two groups. The boys spontaneously began conflicting with each other, for example, taunting each other that 'my group is better than yours'. Sherif put them in competition with each other in sporting activities. This heightened the aggression: they attacked each other more and one group burnt the opposing group's team mascot.

The conflict was starting to get out of hand, so the researchers figured out a way to change this. They arranged for their bus to break down, so all the boys had to cooperate to push-start the bus. The act of having to come together to achieve a common goal reduced the amount of derogation and conflict between the groups.

brilliant tip

Speeches by politicians often emphasise the need for us to 'all pull together' to achieve a common goal. They know this often works to reduce dissension and conflict. Try using this in your own life – when stuck in the middle of warring parties, find a common goal you all need to achieve, and get people to work on this. It may increase cohesion and reduce fighting.

Remember how quick people are to judge people as 'in-group' or 'out-group'. For team building, take steps to emphasise the 'in-group' commonalities.

Losing your sense of individuality

If you are a member of a group, you can lose your own sense of identity and instead identify with the group. This process is called 'de-individuation'. It can fuel aggression: you follow the group rules and feel less accountable for your actions. This is heightened if your individuality is suppressed or disguised, for example, if you wear the group's uniform. In one experiment, when people were disguised to look anonymous in sinister-looking Ku Klux Klan-type outfits, they were more willing to deliver electric shocks.

De-individuation is not always sinister and can be harnessed for good. In another part of the above experiment, when people were dressed in nurses' uniforms, they delivered fewer electric shocks than when they wore their own clothes.

Does power corrupt?

Discoveries about sometimes sinister group processes made psychologists ask the question: what happens when one group has power over another?

In another classic study, Philip Zimbardo set up a mock prison at a university and divided volunteer students into 'prisoners' and 'guards'. He made the prison as realistic as possible, with a uniform for the guards and the prisoners in a knee-length smock, no underwear and their ankles tied together. Within two days, the 'guards' began taking their roles too seriously, forcing the prisoners to strip, do push-ups, clean toilets with their bare hands, and sleep on concrete. Concerned about the prisoners' safety, at the prompting of his girlfriend, Zimbardo had to call off the experiment after six days although it was supposed to last two weeks.

Zimbardo's conclusion was that if you give one group power over another, it inevitably breeds violence and abuse. However, critics said it was due to the set-up, which began with the encouragement of dominance and abuse. So his experiment was recreated by psychologists for a BBC programme. This time there were no suggestions about domination and participants were simply assigned roles. But the results were hardly more encouraging. The prisoners overthrew the guards and tried to establish a peaceful democracy, but when this failed the 'new guards' wanted to establish a regime that was just as tyrannical as the original Stanford experiment. Seeing the direction things were heading, the experimenters again ended the project prematurely.

A reason for optimism

Violence is not something inexplicable or just the actions of a few evil, disturbed or psychopathic personalities, groups or nations. The harm we inflict on each other springs from psychological motivations that are found in all of us.

But the high rate of violence does not mean it is inevitable. In his book *The Better Angels of our Nature*, Steven Pinker explains why and how the rate of violence has declined worldwide, but especially in the West. Murder, rape and war have dramatically decreased because of multiple factors including better government, international trade, law and order, and education.

We see the psychology of competition and conflict in play every day – in office politics, people fighting for a seat on the train, brawls in bars, reports of violence and war in the news. But the place where we can feel the tension between competition and cooperation the most is in the home: the battle of the sexes.

brilliant recap

- At the heart of human life is a fundamental tension: while it pays to cooperate, it also pays to cheat and harm others.
- We probably have an innate talent for spotting social cheats.
- Our superior cognitive abilities make us masters of deception.
- Much human violence is committed by ordinary people because of mundane social forces such as norms for obedience.
- Other motivations for violence are emotion, ideology and in-group and out-group competition.
- When one group has power over another it is a breeding ground for oppression.

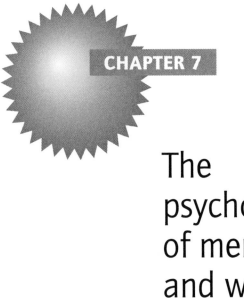

The psychology of men and women

Nature has equipped men and women with different bodies, but do we have different minds? The idea that 'Men are from Mars, Women are from Venus' is a popular one and some psychologists believe there are innate differences between the sexes. But the topic is highly controversial.

What are women good at?

Psychologist Simon Baron-Cohen believes that, on average, women are better at empathising than men. So they have superior skills in both:

- cognitive empathy: the ability to 'read' the minds of others
- affective empathy: the ability to feel the appropriate emotion in response to others.

Baron-Cohen believes this ability to tune into other people's feelings and thoughts gives women better people skills. Their superior empathy means they are more effective communicators, are better at anticipating other people's needs and good at initiating and sustaining relationships. According to Baron-Cohen, this explains why women are generally less aggressive than men. Their greater capacity for empathy means they are more likely to 'feel' the distress caused by the infliction of violence. He argues that women have a natural advantage and interest in roles which require a high level of empathy, for example, therapists, nurses, personnel, mediators and teachers.

Why should women be better at empathising? Baron-Cohen believes this sex difference is a result of evolutionary forces. Empathy is an advantage in providing good care to children. A child with a mother attuned to his or her needs was more likely to survive and to develop a better attachment relationship. He also argues that cooperation is more important for women. Women have a greater need to rely on others due to their greater burden of childcare. So women with superior people skills were better at making and keeping friends and were more likely to thrive.

Women also needed mindreading abilities to cope with men. The ones who were good at spotting liars were less likely to be fooled by men who faked the sincerity of their intentions at the beginning of a prospective sexual relationship. The ability to read emotions was an advantage for dealing with male aggression: it meant they could sense threat and takes steps to protect themselves. They used their skills to maintain a relationship with their children's father, who could provide food and protection.

Baron-Cohen also suggests that women developed better language abilities than men because their survival depended more on skills in the strategic use of language in making friends and dealing with enemies.

exercise How empathic are you?

Baron-Cohen has devised a questionnaire to give us our Empathy Quotient. You can also see how you score on the 'reading the mind in the eyes test'. This measures your ability to guess somebody's state of mind by just looking at the expression in their eyes. Women tend to score more highly than men on both of these measures. These tests are available online at: http://glennrowe.net/BaronCohen.aspx

If you score highly in the Empathy Quotient test then you may have what Baron-Cohen calls brain type 'E'. Although women are more likely to have this brain type, Baron-Cohen emphasises that many men will also have brain type 'E'.

What are men good at?

Baron-Cohen believes that, on the whole, men are better at 'systemising'. This is the ability to analyse or construct a system.

A system is anything that follows rules and has inputs and outputs. So a car is a system where the input is petrol and the output is speed, and it follows the rules of engineering. Systems can be natural, such as a plant, with inputs of sunlight and outputs of growth that follow the rules of biological processes, or abstract, such as in mathematics or computer programming. Baron-Cohen also says men have better spatial skills because systemising requires the ability to visualise.

So Baron-Cohen's theory is that men are more interested in and better at discovering how systems work. The advantage of systemising is that discovering causes and effects leads to increased control and mastery of the environment. He argues that men will have more natural ability and interest in roles that require more systemising and less empathy, for example, plumbers, electricians, programmers, architects, engineers and mathematicians.

Why should men be better at systemising? Baron-Cohen says the ability to figure out how things worked gave men an advantage in their role as hunters and trackers and led to new ways to make and use tools. Low empathy and greater aggression were advantageous for increasing status in the dominance hierarchy and attracting mates.

↗ exercise   How good at systemising are you?

Baron-Cohen has constructed a Systemising Quotient measure, also available at http://glennrowe.net/BaronCohen.aspx

On average, men score better on this test than women. If your score is high then you may have what Baron-Cohen calls brain type 'S'. Again, he emphasises that although on average more men have this brain type, many women will also have brain type 'S'.

If you are good at both empathising and systemising, then Baron-Cohen says you have a balanced brain, or brain type 'B'.

According to Baron-Cohen's ideas, the communication between the sexes is often problematic because men try to figure out women as if they were a system with predictable inputs and outputs governed by rules. Baron-Cohen says this sort of systemising ability gets you nowhere in trying to understand a person. To understand a person you need to have insight into their mental states, their feelings, intentions and thoughts. These are constantly shifting and dependent on the subtleties of the context, and do not follow 'if-then' rules.

brilliant example

Ben's girlfriend, Michelle, was annoyed with him for booking a fishing trip with his friends when her parents were due to visit. So, to make amends, he took her out for a meal in a romantic restaurant. She was touched and forgave him. Not long after, she was upset with him again: this time he had forgotten about some important exams she was sitting at work. So he booked a meal in the same restaurant again by means of apology. This time she was not impressed. He was mystified – why didn't it work this time?

Ben was trying to figure out Michelle by seeing her as a system with predictable inputs and outputs governed by rules: 'If Upset Girlfriend, then add input of Favourite Romantic Restaurant, to produce output of Happy Girlfriend'. But understanding Michelle required empathy and insight into the fact that she was feeling hurt by his continued failure to take account of her feelings and needs.

Are men and women really from 'different planets'?

Research reveals a range of differences between the sexes, for example:

Men

- Two-year-old boys prefer to play with mechanical-type toys rather than dolls.
- Boys have poorer social skills, for example, when joining a new group of children, boys are likely to jump in and try to change the play activity.
- Men perform better on some tests of mathematical problem-solving.
- Men perform better at spatial rotation tasks.

Women

- Girls begin to talk a month earlier than boys, their vocabulary is larger, they are better spellers and readers and have better verbal memory.
- Two-year-old girls are more interested in playing with dolls than mechanical toys.
- Girls show better social skills, for example, when joining a new group of children, girls take time to observe what the group is doing and then take part in whatever is happening.
- Women talk about mental states more than men, and they are more likely to use words such as 'know', 'think', 'want', 'assume', 'intend', 'desire', 'believe', 'imagine', 'pretend', 'expect', 'understand', 'remember' or 'realise'.

- In studies of personality, women score more highly on agreeableness, the personality trait associated with empathy, cooperation and social skill, than men. The average man scores lower on agreeableness than 70 per cent of women.

Male and female aggression

Men are more physically aggressive than women. Boys show more 'rough-housing' play than girls, for example, when playing with a toy car, boys are more likely to ram into each other, whereas girls will avoid bumping into people.

At the extreme end of the violence spectrum, in all societies, men are far more likely to murder than women. Men killing men is 30 to 40 times more frequent than women murdering women. Much male aggression is about fighting for a place in the dominance hierarchy, as discussed in Chapter 6, as about two-thirds of male homicides are fights over being 'disrespected'.

Although males are far more physically aggressive, research shows that if you include verbal aggression, then women are not exactly blameless. Psychologists observed adolescents and found that although boys were more likely to hit and kick each other, girls did just as much shouting and name calling.

Girls are more likely to use more subtle forms of aggression towards people, such as spreading rumours about them, telling their secrets and encouraging people to ostracise them. The female dominance hierarchy exists, but it is a bit more subtle. Females show their dominance by ignoring someone, refusing eye contact and using veiled 'put-downs' so they can deny hostile intent if necessary.

Simon Baron-Cohen says female aggression makes use of more advanced mind-reading skills. Because women are attuned to other people's minds, they know how to hurt by more subtle psychological means.

But is Baron-Cohen right?

Some psychologists are highly sceptical about Baron-Cohen's claims. Cordelia Fine, in her book *Delusions of Gender*, is highly critical of the SQ and EQ questionnaires. She says all they measure is people's views of sex stereotypes. When you answer the questions you know the expectations attached to your gender, so you rate yourself accordingly. If you are a man you rate yourself as better on systemising abilities; if you are a woman you rate your empathising abilities highly.

brilliant insight

The magical disappearing sex differences

Research reveals that men are capable of just as much empathy as women – if it pays. When men were rewarded for empathy, their scores were no different to women's. Another study showed when you tell men that getting in touch with their 'feminine side' makes them more attractive to women and more successful at getting them into bed, they perform just as well on empathy measures. Cordelia Fine concludes that the idea of innate male insensitivity 'is a bit of a myth'.

Studies also reveal that women are just as good at spatial and maths tasks as men – when they believe they are. Researchers told a group of people that females are better at mental rotation tasks than men. When they carried out the tasks, there was no difference in performance between males and females. In another study, researchers told people there were no sex differences in aptitude for maths. When tested, the women actually outperformed the men.

Fine argues that men and women are brought up to have different self-concepts and they behave according to their expectations of themselves. So a negative view of women's spatial and maths abilities becomes a self-fulfilling prophecy. When women carry out a task that goes against the stereotype,

> men and women are brought up to have different self-concepts

for example take a maths test, they become anxious about performing badly, known as 'stereotype threat'. This anxiety then interferes with concentration and interferes with performance.

Fine also points out that just because sex differences can be observed in very young children, does not necessarily mean they are 'hardwired'. Expectations of boys and a girl are different from birth. For example, researchers analysed birth announcements in newspapers and found a difference in the way emotions were expressed at the birth of a boy or girls. Parents were more likely to say they were 'proud' at the birth of a boy than of a girl. From the beginning, achievement and social standing is associated more with boys. So very young children pick up on role expectations for boys and girls and behave accordingly.

Cordelia Fine and others believe it is time to stop looking for 'hardwired' differences in ability between men and women. This line of enquiry reinforces sex stereotypes which are likely to amplify sex differences in performance, as well as encourage sex discrimination. Even if there is a small difference between the sexes in ability as a group, this does not help us predict any individual man or woman's performance.

Sexual attraction

Why do we fancy some people but not others? We might like to think that physical appearance is not the most crucial factor. In surveys, most people say that looks are not the most important reason for whether or not they are attracted to someone. But research suggests that we are kidding ourselves.

When people are set up by psychologists to go on 'dates', study after study shows that physical attractiveness is the most important factor in determining whether they would be interested in seeing their 'date' a second time.

And if we try and comfort ourselves with the idea that there is a huge diversity in what is considered 'attractive', then we will be disappointed again. People from different races and cultures show a surprisingly high level of agreement on what they consider to be physically attractive. Although we might think our desire for good looks is due to brainwashing from a beauty-obsessed Western culture, according to surveys people in non-Western cultures place even more importance on looks in a partner.

Psychologist Nancy Etcoff points to the findings on human beauty. We all prefer symmetrical faces and bodies, clear skin and a youthful appearance. Signs of attractiveness in women are big, widely spaced eyes, plump lips, a small nose and a delicate jaw. The attractive body shape for a woman is a hip to waist ratio of 0.7 with the waist being 70 per cent as wide as the hips. Etcoff and others believe this is because these features are signs of youthfulness and fertility, and signal a high level of oestrogen.

Women are attracted to men who are tall, with a narrow waist and wide shoulders, broad chest and square jaws, and an angular face, cues that they are strong, healthy and have high levels of testosterone.

brilliant insight

The beauty prejudice

It may come as no surprise to learn that beautiful people have an advantage from birth. As seen in Chapter 1, mothers pay more attention to pretty babies than plain babies, and less attractive children are at greater risk of being abused. This discrimination continues into adulthood: good-looking people are perceived as being kinder, more intelligent, honest and trustworthy, and judges are more lenient to them in court. Nice-looking people find partners more easily and beautiful women are more likely to find a partner with a higher status and more wealth than themselves.

However, studies show that beautiful people do not have everything. Good looks do not correspond highly with self-esteem, and attractiveness is not linked highly with happiness.

Although research shows we prefer good looks, we tend to end up with partners who have a similar level of attractiveness to ourselves. This is the 'matching hypothesis' – we select people we feel are our equals in looks to avoid the likelihood of rejection. Most people are realistic and stay in their 'league'.

Similarity attracts in other ways, too. Married and dating couples tend to be similar in age, race, religion, social class, education, intelligence and attitudes.

> something we all find attractive are the signs that someone likes us too

Something we all find attractive are the signs that someone likes us too. A well-known finding is that we are more attracted to people when they have dilated pupils, even though we do not consciously notice this fact. Why is this? Our pupils dilate when we like the look of something. So our unconscious registers that this is a person who is attracted to us, and we are more positively disposed towards them.

Love on the internet

Meeting a partner online is becoming increasingly common. What psychological differences are there in meeting people online rather than face to face?

One difference is that because the other person is not present, people use their imaginations instead to 'fill in the gaps' of what the person is like. This can create a powerful attraction, which may be based far more on fantasy than reality.

When people get to know each other online, their relationship develops more rapidly. Relationships progress through increased self-disclosure, and people tend to open up more quickly on the internet. Because their partner is miles away, the risks are smaller – they can exit the conversation with just a key stroke. The problem is that this 'eroticised pseudo-intimacy' is not based on a solid foundation of knowledge, and obviously the potential for deception is much greater online.

Perhaps because of this accelerated intimacy, people seem to be less cautious about relationships which started on the internet. Research shows that the chance of them having sex without condoms is much higher. Commitment seems to be quicker when people meet through online dating agencies: one study found that the courtships lasted 18 months before marriage rather than the usual 42 months.

Despite this lack of caution, research also suggests people who met on the internet are just as satisfied in their relationship as those who met in real life. Whether these relationships are more or less likely to end in divorce is too early to say.

What women want

Psychologist David Buss has made extensive studies of male and female sexual partner preferences. He says 'much of what I discovered about human mating is not nice'.

For example, in a survey of 10,000 people from 37 different cultures, he discovered that women have a consistent preference for men with high status and money. Women will find a man more sexually attractive if he looks rich. Research shows that women rate the same man as being more attractive if he is in a suit and wearing a Rolex than when wearing a Burger King uniform. And women are far more likely to respond to singles ads if the man has stated he is well-off.

What men want

Men do not care about status and money: this does not enhance a woman's attractiveness. Instead, they care about youthfulness and good looks. Men are far more likely to reply to a singles ad if the woman has stated she is young and physically attractive.

Why do men and women look for different things? Evolutionary psychologists believe these preferences have a biological basis. Women invest more personal resources into their children, the 'parental investment' theory. Childbearing and breastfeeding is demanding, and women who chose men who provided better resources were more likely to see their children survive. Men who preferred fertile, healthy women as sexual partners had more children than those who preferred older women past childbearing age.

The 'kindness dilemma'

Of course, people do not just care about looks and money, they value other qualities as well, such as kindness. Psychologist Daniel Nettle says this poses a dilemma for women who want social status from a partner as well as kindness. Personality research suggests that people who rise high on the ladder of success are likely to have low scores in agreeableness and to show more Machiavellian and psychopathy traits.

'The kind of person who could give you a glittering lifestyle is quite likely not the kind of person you would wish to share such a life with.'

Daniel Nettle

Can a GSOH laugh you into bed?

One of the most common requests in a singles ad is 'must have a GSOH'. Psychologist Geoffrey Miller believes a good sense of humour is important for us not only because it is entertaining and makes us feel good, but because it is a sign of creativity, energy and intelligence.

In one recent study, women read brief descriptions written by men, some of which were very funny and others less so. The women said they were more likely to enter a relationship with the funnier men and rated them as more intelligent.

Men also say they prefer women with a good sense of humour. But research suggests this is not the case – when put to the test, men do not rate funnier women as more attractive.

Geoffrey Miller, in his book *The Mating Mind*, even proposes that our preference for witty, clever and creative partners is the reason for our existence as a species. According to Miller, we inherited bigger brains because the people with interesting minds were more likely to attract sexual partners. He thinks the brain is like the peacock's tail – a showy organ that attracts mates. He believes the human mind is 'an entertainment system designed to stimulate other brains'.

The wide range of human sexuality

Much of the psychological research about the factors that make men and women desirable has focused on heterosexual relationships rather than same sex attraction.

Based on the findings of his pioneering research in the 1940s and 1950s, famous sexologist Alfred Kinsey proposed that sexual orientation is on a continuum. He categorised sexual behaviour on a seven-point scale:

0 – Exclusively heterosexual behaviour

1 – Predominantly heterosexual, only incidental homosexual behaviour

2 – Predominantly heterosexual, more than incidental homosexual behaviour

3 – Equal amount of homosexual and heterosexual behaviour

4 – Predominantly homosexual, more than incidental heterosexual behaviour

5 – Predominantly homosexual, only incidental heterosexual behaviour

6 – Exclusively homosexual behaviour

Another category 'X' was added later, for people who are asexual, that is those who are not sexually attracted to either men or women, thought to be about 1 per cent of the population.

The fact that human beings are attracted to the same sex does not mark us out from the rest of the animal kingdom. Homosexual behaviour in males and females has been observed in as many as 1,500 species, such as whales, giraffes, dolphins and apes. About 10 per cent of domestic rams are exclusively homosexual. Bonobo chimps, one of our closest genetic relatives, are thought to almost all show bisexual behaviour.

sexual orientation can change through a person's life

Typically, our feelings of attraction to the same sex, to the opposite sex, or to both commence about three years before we become sexually active. Sexual orientation can change through a person's life, and women's sexuality seems to be particularly plastic with women reporting more changes over their lifetime in their attraction to the same or opposite sex.

No one knows why people should have one sexuality over another. A person's identification with the same or other sex parent has no influence on whether they become straight, gay or bisexual. The first sexual encounter also has no bearing on whether people become straight or gay, indicating that sexuality is not something you learn from your first sexual experience. Like every other aspect of human behaviour, sexuality is determined by a combination of heritable and environmental factors.

The isolation, stress, low social support, victimisation and rejection that many gay, lesbian and bisexual people experience can make them more vulnerable to anxiety, depression and suicide. However, those who do not experience victimisation and isolation are no more likely to be anxious or depressed than anyone else.

One of the websites developed to tackle discrimination has contributions, amongst others, from Barack Obama: www. itgetsbetter.org

Do you continually think about sex?

Sex surveys confirm the common belief that men are generally more interested in sex than women. One survey found that 54 per cent of men reported that they thought about sex every day, compared to 19 per cent of women. Men spend more money on sexual entertainment, rate their sex drive as being higher, and initiate sex more often.

Women are, on the whole, more choosy about sexual partners. This makes sense according to the 'parental investment' theory, because women have more to lose from picking someone who will abandon them, and can only have a small number of children.

brilliant example

According to the stereotype, men are willing to engage in casual sex more than women, and women are more choosy. To find out if this was true, male and female researchers struck up a conversation with an opposite sex stranger on a college campus and asked them if they would like to have sex.

And the results? Seventy-five per cent of the men were happy to take up this invitation. The number of women who said yes: zero.

However, the differences between men and women may be less marked than they first appear. When it comes to picking a long-term partner both men and women are equally choosy. If a man is going to invest in a woman long term he will find the best person he can get.

Friends with benefits

Differences in male-female preference may have been shaped by our evolutionary past, but of course times have changed and we are not slaves to our DNA.

Sexual relationships with just friendship and without love or expectation of commitment are becoming increasingly common, at least according to a study of college campuses in the US: 50 to 60 per cent of people reported they had been involved in a 'friends with benefits' relationship.

But males and females were subtly different in their attitudes to these relationships.

Researchers found that men and women saw them differently: women said these arrangements had a high level of emotional involvement and they emphasised the friendship benefit. Men, on the other hand, saw the relationship as being casual and emphasised the sexual benefit.

Sexual fantasy

The majority, about 70 per cent, of men and women say they fantasise when having sex. The quality of the fantasy tends to differ. Men focus on explicit sexual acts, whereas women include more social and emotional content and include more 'setting' and 'build up' in their fantasies.

Sexual domination and submission is a common theme in both men's and women's fantasies. It is not well understood why this should be, but the parts of the brain involved in domination and submission are close to those involved with pleasure. In the animal kingdom, domination and submission often form part of the mating ritual.

Most women have difficulties in climaxing during penetrative sex, and need additional, direct stimulation of the clitoris. Women usually take longer to orgasm. According to research by Masters and Johnson, on average a man takes four minutes to climax and a woman ten to twenty minutes.

The female orgasm is usually more elusive than a man's. Psychologist George Miller sees this as another aspect of women's greater sexual choosiness.

Women do not respond as easily to sexual stimulation unless the conditions are right and they feel comfortable about the man's personality and intentions. Miller believes female sexuality is wired to show more discrimination and he calls this 'the choosy clitoris'.

What is 'normal'?

Of course, lots of people do not fit these generalisations. Many men are very choosy about their sexual partners, many women are not. Many men find it difficult to climax, lots of women do not. Perhaps even more than in any other aspect of life, people want to feel they are 'normal' with regards to sex. If you define normal as conforming to what most people do, this depends on the population or culture in which you live. Sexual behaviour is so varied that perhaps the best thing that could be said is that 'variation is normal': it is normal to be different.

> people want to feel they are 'normal' with regards to sex

The internet pornography controversy

Many people are worried about the effect of the widespread availability of pornography on the internet. The volume and range of instantly accessible material is unprecedented in human history. One concern is that pornography encourages the kind of attitudes that lead to sexual violence. But, despite the increasing availability of pornography, the incidence of rape has decreased in Western countries in recent years.

Whether or not pornography encourages sexual violence, it may cause problems in other ways. After looking at pornographic images, men rated their partners as being less attractive and felt less in love with their wives. Pornography can be addictive, with some men spending so much time looking at internet images that their work, social and family lives suffer. One study found that porn use can turn men off sex altogether – they become so desensitised to erotic images that they no longer respond to sexual stimulation.

Pornography is also probably causing body image dissatisfaction in women. More women are requesting genital surgery, feeling that to look 'normal' they have to look like a porn star.

We do not know what the long-term impact is of internet pornography on young people. The cohort of teenagers from a few years ago, the first to have easy access to huge quantities of porn, are not yet at an age when people typically settle down into longer-term relationships. In a sense, we are near the beginning of a long-term experiment in human sexuality and we do not yet know whether it will have favourable or adverse consequences.

The psychology of romantic love

Sexual attraction might or might not turn into love. Psychology research shows that falling in love is the same experience for all of us, whatever our sex, age, race or sexuality. We are gripped by passion, our energy levels sky rocket and our mood swings from elation to despair. Love hijacks our cognitive functioning with intrusive thoughts and obsessive focus about our loved one. We are blind to their shortcomings and put them on a pedestal to an extent that is almost delusional. Inspired by the beloved, we take on new interests, values and attitudes.

Researcher Helen Fisher wanted to find what was going on in our brains during this process. She placed an advert saying 'Have you just fallen madly in love?' and recruited couples, putting them under a brain scanner. She discovered that 'loved-up' minds were very active in the caudate nucleus. This is a primitive region in the centre of our brains, part of the 'reward' system that drives our motivations to act. Fisher concluded that romantic love is not simply an emotion, but is a fundamental drive. She says it is a passion that comes from the 'motor of the mind'. We have basic motivation to form these bonds, to hold men and women together long enough for successful childrearing.

> romantic love is not simply an emotion, but is a fundamental drive

brilliant tip

Helen Fisher says doing new and exciting things together with your partner can help keep your love alive. Researchers found that couples who carried out an exciting activity together rated their love as stronger afterwards.

The mystery of love

But why do people fall in love with one person and not another? One theory is that people have an 'ideal' partner in their minds, and fall in love with those who match up to the ideal. Studies of couples show the closer a partner measured up to their ideals, the more satisfied they were with the relationship. Researchers can predict whether couples would continue dating or not by looking at the size of the discrepancy between their ideals and the reality.

Can love be analysed into components? Psychologists have tried. Robert Sternberg proposes that love, like hate, has three aspects:

1 Intimacy: the feelings of closeness, warmth, concern for each other's well-being and sense of connection.

2 Passion: intense romantic feelings and sexual attraction, the cravings to be physically close and sexual with the person.

3 Commitment: the conscious decision to stay with the person despite any difficulties which may arise.

Sternberg says the quality of love in a relationship depends on the presence or absence of each of the components, producing different love styles, for example:

- Infatuation: This is where only passion is felt, and is unlikely to last long without intimacy or commitment.

- Companionate love: intimacy and commitment without passion.

- Empty love: Where only commitment is present. This may happen at the end of a relationship, when intimacy and passion have gone.

- Consummate love: Where the couple feel all three components: intimacy, passion and commitment. This is the kind of love many people hope to find.

An alternative way of looking at love: attachment

Another way of understanding love is to look at how the 'internal working models' of the relationships you developed in childhood influence your adult love life. According to this view, proposed by Hazan and Shaver, your adult attachment style tends to follow the same pattern as the attachments you had as a child.

There are two main dimensions in your attachment style, described by Kim Bartholomew and Leonard Horowitz. The first is how anxious you are. People high in anxiety are worried about whether they are really loved, and are afraid of abandonment – their internal working models of how relationships work are dominated by anxiety. The second dimension is how avoidant you are. This is the degree to which you are comfortable with getting close to others.

These two dimensions combine to form basic attachment styles in four quadrants:

Attachment styles

Source: Based on Bartholomew & Horovitz (1991)

exercise

Read the attachment styles below, described by Bartholomew and Horowitz. Which one fits you best?

1   It is easy for me to become emotionally close to others. I am comfortable depending on others and having others depend on me. I don't worry about being alone or having others not accept me.

2 I am comfortable without close emotional relationships. It is important to me to feel independent and self-sufficient, and I prefer not to depend on others or have others depend on me.

3 I want to be completely emotionally intimate with others, but I often find others are reluctant to get as close as I would like. I am uncomfortable being without close relationships, but I sometimes worry that people don't value me as much as I value them.

4 I am uncomfortable getting close to others. I want emotionally close relationships, but I find it difficult to trust others completely, or depend on them. I worry that I will be hurt if I allow myself to get too close to others.

If you feel you relate more to (1) then you are secure – low anxiety and low avoidance; (2) is dismissing – low anxiety and high avoidance; (3) is preoccupied; (4) is fearful.

You can take a questionnaire to measure you attachment style at: http://www.web-research-design.net/cgi-bin/crq/crq.pl

Research on attachment styles in adults show that 'secure' people report having more stable and satisfying relationships, and are less likely to suffer from depression. Insight into your own and your partner's attachment style can tell you how easily you will fulfil each other's needs. For example, a person who is very anxious in relationships is a poor fit with someone who is very avoidant. The anxious person will crave more closeness and the avoidant person will pull away.

Similar to the behaviour of children when they are separated from their parents, when an adult's attachment is ruptured love often turns to fury. This is known as 'abandonment rage'. As people instinctively realise, the emotions of love and hate are closely related. Neuroscience seems to back this up – love and hate use similar circuits in the brain.

The psychology of a happy relationship

Thankfully, not all love relationships end in hatred and abandonment. So why do some couples stay together?

Psychologist John Gottman has studied hundreds of couples and has found that those who stay together have a ratio of at least five positive interactions to each negative one. So positive interactions – like compliments, showing affection and concern, sharing jokes and experiences – need to outnumber the complaints, bickering and cold shoulder treatment.

The way people handle conflict is also important. Couples who break up show four types of behaviour during an argument – Gottman calls them the 'four horsemen of the apocalypse' because they spell doom for the relationship:

1 Criticism – complaining by attacking their loved one's personality, such as saying 'you are lazy'.

2 Contempt – non-verbal signs such as sneering, eye rolling, saying things to imply their partner is inferior as a person, for example 'you are a waste of space'.

3 Defensiveness – arguing back at everything, without considering different perspectives, denying any culpability.

4 Stonewalling – withdrawing from the argument, not responding properly or ignoring their partner, who feels like they are talking to a wall.

According to Gottman's research, when people continue to show all these signs in their arguments, there is over a 99 per cent chance they will break up.

brilliant dos and don'ts

How to reduce the conflict in your relationship – tips from John Gottman's research:

DO

✔ *Use a softened start-up*

If you want to bring up a difficult topic or point of conflict, do it gently, what Gottman calls a 'softened start-up'. If you begin on a soft note, there is a good chance you will resolve the problem together.

✔ *Make repair attempts*

Happy couples say something that show they care, or make a self-deprecating joke during arguments, known as 'repair attempts'. These lower the emotional temperature of the argument and help prevent it from escalating.

✔ *Accept influence from each other*

In successful relationships, couples take each other's feelings and perspectives into account when making decisions, what Gottman calls 'accepting influence'.

✔ *Act like a best friend*

Show the same consideration, kindness and respect to your partner that you would to a good friend. Gottman found that relationship satisfaction is closely linked to the quality of the friendship the couple have with each other.

DON'T

✗ *Use a harsh start-up*

If you raise a difficult topic or point of conflict by making a criticism or hostile comment, the argument will end badly. Gottman says he can predict 96 per cent of the time how a conflict will end by looking at the first three minutes.

X **Let the argument escalate out of control**
Happier couples recognise when things are getting too heated
and agree to exit the discussion and come back to it after
calming down.

X **Make unilateral decisions**
Failing to give your partner a say in decisions which affect you
both will have a very negative effect on the relationship. Men
in particular have a problem in 'accepting influence' from their
wives or girlfriends, and when this is the case the relationship is
less likely to last.

X **Voice every negative feeling**
Resist the temptation to blurt out all the hurtful comments
that come to mind during an argument. Happier couples 'edit'
themselves during difficult conversations.

*'Happily married couples behave like good friends, and deal with
conflict in gentle, positive ways.'*

The Gottman Relationship Institute

Are same sex relationships easier?

Gottman says that although same sex couples show similar patterns in their relationships, gay and lesbian couples deal better
with conflict. They keep their sense of humour better, show
more affection during an argument and take it less personally if
their partner criticises them. They are also less likely to use controlling and hostile tactics with each other. He concludes that
same sex couples deal better with fairness and power sharing.

Keep hold of the rose-tinted spectacles

How objectively can you see your partner's negative traits and personality flaws?

If you want a long, happy relationship, don't look at them too hard. Researchers assessed people's real life character traits and compared these ratings with their partner's view. Those who held an unrealistically optimistic view of their partner were happier.

Our minds are good at constructing illusions, and this may be a time when we should keep them. The multitude of other ways that our minds play tricks is our next topic.

brilliant recap

- Men and women show some different behaviours, preferences and abilities; some believe these may have an innate component, others point to the power of social expectations.

- One theory is that men are better at 'systemising' and women are better at 'empathising'.

- Research shows that there are consistent differences in terms of sexual partner preferences between men and women.

- Love seems to be a basic biological drive.

- The pattern of your early attachment relationships influences the pattern of your adult love relationships.

- The key to a happy relationship is in ensuring you have more positive interactions than negative, and that you deal with conflict effectively.

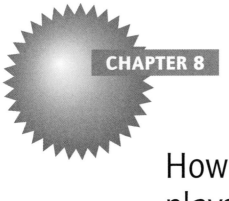

CHAPTER 8

How the mind plays tricks

'Everyone complains about his memory, and no one complains about his judgement.'

Francois de la Rochefoucald, seventeenth-century writer

Most of the time we have the feeling we are experiencing the world as it really is. This is because, as psychologist Daniel Gilbert puts it, your mind does a good job of creating an impression of a continuous, sensible reality.

But occasionally, we have a glimpse into the fact that things are not quite how they seem. For example, look at this picture. You know that white is white and black is black, but...

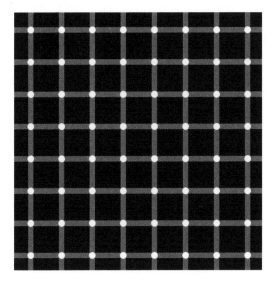

… why do the white dots flit from being white to dark? This illusion, called the 'scintillating grid', is a side effect of how our visual receptor cells fire. If our minds can create black out of white, what other tricks can they play on us?

Our judgement of ourselves

Be honest, do you feel you are above average in:

- intelligence
- driving ability
- getting on well with other people
- sensitivity
- job performance
- honesty
- generosity?

You probably said 'yes' to most, if not all of these. So do most people – we all typically think we are better than average in these things. And, of course, you might be. But somebody has to be below average.

> most people think they are superior to others on all sorts of positive traits

Research shows that most people think they are superior to others on all sorts of positive traits. This is known as the 'Lake Wobegon effect', named after an American radio broadcaster's fictional town where 'the women are strong, the men are good-looking and all the children are above average'.

Suppose you are in hospital after a car crash. Would your conviction that you are a better than average driver be shaken? Probably not: studies have shown people hospitalised after a traffic accident rate their driving skill just as highly as everyone else – even when the accident was their fault.

But we do not all delude ourselves like this. Perhaps you were unsure about your level of intelligence? This might be a good sign. People with high IQs tend to underestimate their intelligence, whereas people with low IQs vastly overestimate theirs.

Unskilled and unaware of it

Perhaps you were less confident about other aspects of your skills, such as your job performance. This, again, might be genuine modesty on your part, and you are much better than you think.

The irony is that those who are the poorest performers are the most deluded about it. This is known as the Dunning-Kruger effect: people who have the lowest level of skill are the least aware of their own incompetence. Studies reveal that the worst performing medical students, lab technicians, readers and chess players are unaware of it. Not only do they have little insight into their own shortcomings, but they are unable to recognise when others are showing skill. When we are particularly bad at something, our minds shield us from the truth.

Delusions of skill

People who invest in stock markets for a living are confident in their skills in predicting prices and knowing when to buy or sell. But research shows even professional investors do little or no better than chance. The proof of skill is consistent performance, but hardly any stock pickers show it – their success fluctuates. Daniel Kahneman concludes that nearly all traders perform no better than if they were rolling dice. He concludes that 'a major industry appears to be built largely on an illusion of skill' and investment firms reward luck as if it was talent. He points to research that shows the most active traders get the worst results – as they act on their wrong ideas more often they lose more money.

If traders have no skill, known as the 'illusion of validity', why do they believe in themselves? It is because they have a 'confirmation bias'. They focus on the times they were successful and pay less attention to the times they were wrong. And when the other traders around them are also convinced of their skill, the social norms are powerful.

'People can maintain an unshakable faith in any proposition, however absurd, when they are sustained by a community of like-minded believers.'

Daniel Kahneman

A wide variety of other professionals are prey to the illusion they have predictive abilities. Kahneman states that experts in politics and economics often perform worse in their predictions than 'dart-throwing monkeys'. Experts in all sorts of areas, from clinical psychology, medicine, the wine trade, football, social work and the prison service are no better at predicting outcomes than if they had just used a quick formula. For example, using a student's previous scores and an aptitude test is a better predictor of academic performance than the judgement of 'experts' who have access to these scores but have also interviewed the student and read a four-page personal statement.

Even people who know they are playing a game of chance cannot help having illusions of validity. This human frailty is exploited by the gambling industry. Problem gamblers are convinced they are skilled at a card game or can predict the roll of the dice, despite all evidence to the contrary.

Profile: Daniel Kahneman

Steven Pinker describes Daniel Kahneman, born 1934, as 'certainly the most important psychologist alive today'. Originally from Israel, Kahneman is a professor at Princeton University in America. During his career he has studied diverse areas of psychology and, together with his colleague Amos Tversky, has pioneered research into human decision-making, which won him a Nobel Prize in economics. Tversky could not share the award as he died in 1996, and the Nobel Prize is not awarded posthumously.

Kahneman and Tversky's work inspired economists to think completely differently about the way we make decisions: we are not rational economic beings but are subject to all sorts of errors and biases. This has had an influence far beyond the narrow confines of academia. Kahneman's colleague, the economist Richard Thaler, argued that policy makers should use psychology to encourage the public to make 'better' decisions. In other words, public and private organisations should 'nudge' us in the right direction by employing strategies that take our psychological processes into account. This is not just for decisions about money, but in all areas of our lives. Richard Thaler and Cass Sunstein describe these in their book, *Nudge: Improving Decisions about Health, Wealth and Happiness.*

These ideas have been taken up by leaders such as Barack Obama and David Cameron. The 'Behavioural Insights Team', known as the 'Nudge Unit', was set up by the Cabinet Office in 2010. This advises on the ways public organisations can help people make 'better' choices, using understanding about human decision-making from Kahneman and Tverksy's work amongst others.

An example of one such 'nudge' is that from October 2012, all workers were automatically enrolled into a pension scheme, and have to make an active choice to opt out of it. Because simple inertia is a big factor in our decision-making, many of us do not sign up for a pension, not because of a rational judgement process, but because it involves cognitive effort.

For more information on how we are being 'nudged' go to: http://www.cabinetoffice.gov.uk/behavioural-insights-team

Illusion of control

Feeling in control is important for most people. A sense of control may even prolong life. Residents in an old people's home who were given control over the timing of their visits from volunteers lived longer than those without control.

Sometimes, though, the sense of control is just a comforting illusion. Ellen Langer asked people to guess how much control they had over a light by pressing a button. People believed they had some control even when the light came on randomly. An example of this in everyday life is when we buy lottery tickets. What do you prefer – to choose your own numbers, or just get random ones? Choosing your own gives no advantage, but research shows we feel more likely to win a lottery if we have chosen the numbers on the ticket.

There are some who do not succumb to this illusion: people who are depressed. Depressed individuals are more accurate in their judgement of control tasks, known as 'depressive realism'.

Self-serving bias: putting ourselves in a good light

Our minds are kind to us. They give explanations of our own behaviour that are generous.

When people are told they have done well on a task, they attribute it to their own skill or personality; when told they have done badly, it is because of circumstance. So when we pass an exam, it is due to our cleverness; if we fail it is because the course was badly taught. But we have the opposite view for other people – when we see someone else making a mistake, we attribute it to their personality, not their circumstances. As seen in Chapter 6, this is the 'fundamental attribution error'. It fuels the sense of injustice behind many pointless conflicts: 'She hit me because she's aggressive, I hit her because the circumstances forced me into defending myself'.

Our minds select information to prop up our self-esteem. Researchers gave students fake feedback, good and bad, about their personalities, such as: 'You would make fun of others because of their looks' and 'You would keep secrets if asked to'. Later on, the students were asked to recall the feedback. They were more likely to remember the positive comments than the negative.

> our minds select information to prop up our self-esteem

How optimistic are you? Are you *correctly* optimistic?

Imagine your future. What will it be like? Do you see better things ahead?

When we contemplate our future, most people imagine it will be an improvement on now, or at least that we will have a better future than other people. We feel we are personally less likely than others to have a car accident, a sexually transmitted disease, cancer, Alzheimer's, a broken bone or a heart attack.

In one experiment, researchers gave students some fake medical results, saying they had a protein deficiency which made them vulnerable to pancreatic disorders in later life. Other students were given a clean bill of health. The ones given the bad news soon decided that protein deficiencies and pancreatic disorders were not particularly serious.

Moreover, when bad news comes along in real life, we preserve our optimism: 96 per cent of cancer patients think they are in better health than the average cancer patient. One study even found that cancer patients were *more* optimistic about their future than healthy people. It seems our own minds are, usually, over-optimistic and deceive us.

Lying to ourselves

We do not just put a positive spin on things, but we tell downright lies to ourselves. In a classic study in the 1950s, experimenters invented tasks that were as pointless and boring as possible, such as turning pegs. After doing the task, they were asked to tell the next person that it was interesting and enjoyable, and were paid either one or twenty dollars for telling this fib.

Later, the experimenters asked participants how much they had really enjoyed the peg-turning task. Which group do you think rated it more enjoyable – those paid one dollar for the lie or those paid twenty dollars?

It was those who had only been paid one dollar. Why is this? They found the task boring, but they told someone it was interesting for a dollar, hardly a worthwhile payment for this amount of dishonesty. When we have incompatible thoughts like this – a feeling we have done something inconsistent with our other beliefs – it creates an unpleasant state of tension, known as 'cognitive dissonance'. Their minds dealt with this dissonance by choosing to remember the task as more enjoyable, thereby reducing the uncomfortable feeling.

When we hold two thoughts or beliefs that are incompatible with each other, our minds will twist facts to reduce the incompatibility. We will believe our own lies because the rearranged facts will fit more neatly together instead of jarring.

Examples of cognitive dissonance in real life are that customers like their kitchen appliances more after they buy them, gamblers think their horse is more likely to win after they have put money on it, and people applying for work rate the job more positively after they have accepted it. Also, there is the phenomenon of 'hazing', where people have to go through an ordeal to join a group. People rate a group more positively if they have to go through a lot of pain or difficulty to join it.

tip

If we struggle to get something, afterwards our minds often assign higher worth to it, because of cognitive dissonance. A lesson from this is that if you want people to value something, do not make it easy for them to get it.

How prone to self-deception are you? Give yourself a score out of ten for how well each of these six statements describe you, where 0 is very inaccurate and 10 is very accurate:

I always know why I do things.

I just know that I will be a success.

I know that my decisions are correct.

I feel comfortable with myself.

I like to take responsibility when making decisions.

I am always honest with myself.

Add up your score, and see where you fit on the scale. The higher your score, the greater your capacity for self-deception.

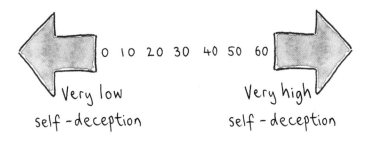

0 10 20 30 40 50 60

Very low
self-deception

Very high
self-deception

Sigmund Freud and the art of self-defence

Why do our minds distort reality so much? Sigmund Freud proposed that our minds are equipped with a variety of defence mechanisms to protect our egos from unpalatable facts about ourselves and the world.

- *Denial*: the well-known defence mechanism whereby we reject the reality of an unpleasant fact, or minimise its importance.

- *Rationalisation*: also made popular by Freud, where our minds consciously or unconsciously justify our actions to make our behaviour seem more acceptable.

- *Reaction formation*: This is one of Freud's more controversial defence mechanisms. Instead of letting ourselves experience unacceptable feelings, we have the extreme opposite reaction. For example, the mother with hostile feelings towards her child behaves in an extremely loving way, but in 'showy' and exaggerated fashion.

Denial and rationalisation are both well-documented, and there is some evidence for reaction formation. Researchers showed pictures of men having sex to a group of heterosexual males. The ones with the most homophobic attitudes showed the most sexual arousal to the pictures. Apparently, the homophobic men were attracted to other men, but this showed itself as hostility instead. Reaction formation remains, however, a controversial concept.

The advantage of lying to ourselves

Freud saw these defence mechanisms as serving adaptive functions, enabling us to get on with our lives rather than being crippled by self-doubt and fear. Other psychologists describe our self-deception in different terms: Daniel Gilbert calls this our 'psychological immune system'.

Robert Trivers also thinks self-deception is a useful survival tool. If you can deceive yourself about the purity of your motives, you will be better at deceiving others. Lying is not easy with a guilty conscience. When your unreliable relative asks for a loan, their protestations that they will pay it back are all the more convincing when they believe it themselves. Anthropologist Lionel Tiger believes our optimism made us the successful species we are.

> self-deception is a useful survival tool

He says without our spirit of recklessness, our ancestors would not have ventured out into new lands and environments, and our attitude of hope made us fight for survival even when the odds looked bad.

Knowing our own feelings

What would be the best way to tell if you'd enjoy going on a blind date with someone?

1 Look at their picture, read their dating profile and decide for yourself.

2 Get the opinion of a person who has already been on a date with them.

Daniel Gilbert found most people would prefer (1), to see the picture and information. But in his research it turned out that getting someone else's opinion was by far the best predictor of whether they would enjoy the date.

We are not very good at predicting how we will feel in the future. This is known as 'affective forecasting'. We are poor judges: it is better to get the opinion of someone who has already been there rather than rely on our guesswork.

brilliant tip

When you are making a decision, ask the opinion of someone who has already experienced the purchase, situation or relationship you are contemplating, and do not be so tempted to dismiss their opinion. Their judgement may well be better than yours.

It's not just forecasting: our memories of *past* feelings are not necessarily very accurate either. Researchers asked men and women to play a competitive word game and record their feelings. At that stage there was no difference in the type or amount of emotions between the men or women.

But a week later they were asked again. Men remembered feeling more 'masculine' emotions during the game, such as anger and pride. Women remembered feeling more 'feminine' ones, such as sympathy and guilt. Their stereotypes about men and women acted like a filter on their memories and changed their recollections.

Do you even know how you feel now?

Can you be sure of your feelings right at this minute? For example, are you happy with your social life right now? When asked this question, most people say they feel reasonably happy.

But with a slight change in wording, you may well give a different answer. When asked 'are you *un*happy with your social life right now?' people say they are less happy. This is the confirmation bias again. We search our memory banks to find the examples that confirm the question. So asked how happy you are with your social life, you think of the positive events: the hilarious lunch with your colleagues, that fantastic 40th birthday party. But when asked about being *un*happy, you think of the dull lunch with your boss or that lonely Friday night in front of the TV with a microwaveable meal-for-one. So our feelings change because of a tiny difference in the wording of a question.

The strange power of 'priming'

We are often blind to the real reasons for our own behaviour.

In one experiment, researchers asked people to unscramble sentences containing a variety of words like 'wrinkle', 'knits', 'forgetful' and 'stubborn' – for example, unscrambling 'sky the seamless grey is a' to form a sentence.

This seemingly straightforward activity had a bizarre effect. After unscrambling these sentences, people were timed as they walked down the corridor on the way out from the test. Was there a difference in walking speeds between subjects who'd unscrambled sentences with words associated with old age, like 'grey' and 'wrinkle', compared to those subjects whose sentences had neutral words?

The answer was yes. Reading words associated with old age had made the participants act 'older'. But when asked why they were walking slowly, they said things like 'I'm tired'. They were completely unaware of the effect.

How does this work? In their minds they had a schema for old people, a set of associations about being elderly. Reading words like 'forgetful' and 'knits' had activated this schema, and because it also includes the concept of being slow it affected their behaviour.

Even a screensaver on a nearby computer can influence your behaviour without you knowing it. Research shows that when people see a screensaver showing images of floating dollar bills, they will sit further away from a stranger. The image of the dollar bills primes their 'money' schema, and the money schema is associated with individualism and self-interest. The sight of money makes people physically distance themselves from others, and be more selfish and less helpful. The researchers also discovered that people 'primed' with money are less likely to help pick up dropped pencils for a stranger.

So can we judge others?

Although we have problems judging ourselves accurately, perhaps we can be more objective and rational about judging other people?

In a classic 1920 study, Edward Thorndike asked commanding officers in the army to rate soldiers on different characteristics, such as intelligence, neatness, physique, leadership ability and honesty. He found that rather than giving different judgements for each trait, the officers rated them similarly on each characteristic. If they had a positive impression in one area, they rated them positively for everything else. This is called the 'halo effect'. Rather than making nuanced and complex judgements of people, we just have an overall negative or positive impression.

Which of the following two men do you like the sound of best?

Alan: intelligent, industrious, impulsive, critical, stubborn, envious.

Ben: envious, stubborn, critical, impulsive, industrious, intelligent.

Solomon Asch posed this question and found that most people prefer Alan. Alan and Ben have the same character traits, but because we see Alan's positive traits first, this initial impression colours our perception of the rest of his personality. Once our judgements of people have formed, they do not change easily.

Experiments on prejudice

We might like to think we have no conscious prejudice against people because of their colour, sexuality, gender or religion. But what about our unconscious? How egalitarian are we deep down?

Researchers have studied this using subliminal exposure techniques. They presented photographs of either black or white faces to people for less than 30 milliseconds, too quick for conscious awareness. Those exposed to pictures of black people showed more hostile behaviour. The photos triggered their schema that black people are aggressive. Research also shows people are likely to mistake an object as a handgun when they have just seen a picture of a black man's face.

This unconscious tendency to react with more hostility to other races can have fatal consequences. In 1999, Amidou Diallo, an unarmed black man, was shot dead while reaching for his wallet. His shooting prompted social psychologists to carry out research into 'shooter bias', and for police to train officers better. However, disproportionate shootings of unarmed black men continue. For example, in 2010, a 27-year-old autistic man Steven Eugene Washington was shot dead by officers who saw him appear to reach towards something in his waistband.

exercise

What prejudices are lurking in your unconscious? To find out, take the online tests at

https://implicit.harvard.edu/implicit/

These tests measure our reaction times when judging other people and reveal our hidden prejudices about race, age, body size, sexuality, religion and gender.

When illusion becomes reality

In a famous experiment, Rosenthal and Jacobson picked out a selection of schoolchildren and told their teacher they would soon perform much better in class. And they turned out to be right: the children did show a big improvement.

research shows that high expectations can bring better performance

But Rosenthal and Jacobson had selected the children completely at random. The teachers believed they would succeed, so they behaved differently to the children and it became a self-fulfilling prophecy. When you ask more from people, you often get more. Research shows that high expectations can bring better performance in teachers, bank employees and military staff.

Self-fulfilling prophecies are not always positive, of course. In a study of behaviour during job interviews, researchers found white interviewers were less friendly with black candidates than white. They kept themselves more distant, made more speech errors and ended the interview more abruptly. The black interviewees performed less well as a consequence.

Afterwards, the interviewers replicated this unfriendly behaviour with the white candidates, too, to see what effect this would have. They discovered that faced with an unfriendly interviewer, the white people performed poorly, too. So our illusions influence our behaviour, have an impact on others and can create a reality of their own.

Our judgement of the world

Here are five strange tricks our minds can play on us:

1 Looked but didn't see

Although we feel as if we are in touch with the reality around us, our focus of attention is so narrow that we miss much of it.

A well-known demonstration of this is the 'invisible gorilla'. This is a video clip of some basketball players and the task is to count the number of passes made by the people in white. During the clip, a man in a gorilla suit walks right across the scene, in full view. About half of people who watch the video do not notice him.

To try a different example of this effect for yourself, go to YouTube and search for 'The monkey business illusion'.

When we focus our attention on one thing, it is almost as if we are blind to everything else. This problem has a serious side: 'looked but didn't see' is one of the most common causes of traffic accidents.

2 Tired and hungry

You are accused of a crime and are up in front of a judge just before lunch, hoping to win parole. We like to think we are cool and objective in our judgements; legal professionals are even more so, surely? The time of day won't make a difference, will it?

Daniel Kahneman presented a study on the way judges make decisions. Just before a meal break the judges turned down all requests for parole. After lunch, they were more benevolent and granted 65 per cent of parole requests. Hungry judges make harsh decisions.

brilliant tip

If you are planning to ask someone for a big favour, make sure they are well-fed first.

3 The lazy brain

Which do you think happens more often: death from accidents or death from diabetes?

Most people say accidents, but the reality is that diabetes kills far more people. Because accidents are more dramatic, fatal events come to our minds more easily, so we assume they are more frequent. This is the 'availability heuristic', discovered by Kahneman and Tversky. Our minds are lazy and tend to make judgements on the information that is easy to retrieve.

Kahneman says this is one reason why bickering couples are always convinced they have done more than their fair share of the household chores. Each person can easily bring to mind all the times he or she did the hoovering, but they find it more difficult to recall their partner doing the same.

4 Loss or gain?

Which of these two would you prefer:

> A ten per cent chance of winning £100, but with a 90 per cent chance of losing £5?
>
> *or*
>
> Buy a lottery ticket for £5 that has a 10 per cent chance to win £100 and a 90 per cent chance of winning nothing?

Kahneman found most people prefer option B. But the two gambles are exactly the same, they both have the same chance of winning or losing the same amount of money. The difference is that option A is framed as a loss. Our minds are averse to loss, so we prefer the option that seems the safest. The way the question is framed has more impact than a logical, mathematical calculation.

Amos Tversky wanted to see if this framing effect affected the way doctors made decisions. He told doctors about survival rates for lung cancer surgery and asked them if they would recommend it for their patients. He framed it as either a gain: 'The one month survival rate is 90 per cent', or as a loss: 'There is 10 per cent mortality in the first month'.

When the survival rates were framed as a gain, the majority of doctors said they would recommend it. When framed as a loss, only half of them chose it. So this effect is not just a quirky laboratory finding – it has implications for the way we make important real-life decisions.

5 Memory

In Chapter 1, we looked at the fallibility of our memory. Daniel Gilbert gives this example to try for yourself. Read the words below:

Bed	Rest
Awake	Tired
Dream	Wake
Snooze	Blanket
Doze	Slumber
Snore	Nap
Peace	Yawn
Drowsy	

Now cover the list with your hand before reading on.

Do you recall reading the word 'gasoline'? Do you remember reading the word 'sleep'?

Most people correctly spot that 'gasoline' was not there, but many falsely remember reading the word 'sleep', which was not on the list. As discussed in Chapter 1, this is because the mind just stores the overall meaning of the word list, not the actual details. We record a general impression and then remember it by 'filling in the blanks' with information we construct later.

This can lead to devastating consequences in real life. If memory is unreliable in a plain word list like the above, imagine how difficult it is to recall real-world events in situations of extreme stress.

The fallibility of memory

In 1984, American university student Jennifer Thompson was brutally attacked and raped by an intruder at knifepoint in her home. During the ordeal she made every effort to memorise the attacker's face. She gave detailed information to the police about his appearance, which was used to make an artist's impression.

A suspect called Ronald Cotton bore a striking resemblance to this picture, and she identified him in a line-up. She said: 'I knew this was the man. I was completely confident.' Her testimony in court was so convincing that Cotton was sentenced to life imprisonment, although he always protested his innocence.

Years later, it emerged that a prisoner called Bobby Poole had been telling his cellmates he was the one who had really committed the attack. But when Poole was shown to Jennifer she swore she had never seen him before. It was only when DNA technology came into use that Bobby Poole was proven guilty. Cotton was finally released, after 11 years in jail for a crime he did not commit.

When Jennifer Thompson was constructing the artist's impression of the attacker's face, her recall was not very accurate. But once the picture had been drawn, it became fixed in her mind as if it was a memory.

After Ronald Cotton's release, he and Jennifer Thompson became unlikely friends and wrote a book together about their experiences. They both campaign for reform in the use of eyewitness testimony in the legal system.

We tend to think that the ultimate proof is seeing something with our own eyes, but once it is stored in our constructive memories, it can be poor evidence indeed.

The biggest illusion of them all?

Although our minds play tricks, one thing we do feel sure of is that we are in charge. We have the power of choice. It was your conscious, reasoning self who made the decision to pick up this text and to be reading these words right now.

A moment's thought though reveals this is not strictly true. Our bodies often move of their own accord when our conscious minds are elsewhere. For example, you walk into the kitchen and you cannot remember why you went there. Or you set off to visit a friend and you realise you have started driving on the familiar route to work instead.

At times our automatic processes control our decisions. But this is so familiar, we do not worry about it. We go into auto-pilot mode to free our conscious minds for important decisions. Most of the time our autopilot gets it right and does more or less what we want.

Our conscious minds seem to make the executive decisions. For example, you could decide right now to either carry on reading this chapter or get on with something else. Your conscious mind is in charge. The unconscious is a useful servant, but we are the ultimate boss. Or are we?

In a famous serious of experiments, scientist Benjamin Libet scanned the brains of people making decisions about simple finger movements. He asked them to press a button whenever they felt like it and to note the exact time that they became aware of the intention to move their finger.

He found there was brain activity in the motor cortex about a third of a second *before* the people consciously decided to move their finger. Their unconscious minds were preparing the action before the conscious mind was aware of its intention to do so.

This implies that our feeling of free will is an illusion. All the decisions have been made down below, at the unconscious level, and the unconscious mind just keeps our conscious minds informed and lets us think we are in charge.

our feeling of free will
is an illusion

So a miracle our mind may be, but at the same time it is lazy, deceitful and self-serving. And that is not the only set of difficulties in possessing an intelligent, conscious mind. All too often, our minds seem to turn against us and give us a whole myriad of psychological problems, the subject of the next chapter.

brilliant recap

- We believe we have above average abilities, and those of us who have the least talent are the least aware of it.

- We believe we have skill and that we are in control when we are not; there are many well-paid professionals who are rewarded for performing no better than chance.

- We are prone to all sorts of self-serving biases that preserve our self-esteem.

- We are poor judges of our own internal world, with little insight into our behaviours and motivations.

- We hold unconscious prejudices which affect our own and others' behaviour and can become a self-fulfilling prophecy.

- Even our sense of free will may be an illusion.

CHAPTER 9

Understanding psychological problems

At least a quarter of us will suffer some kind of psychological problem. It is normal for us to experience problems in the way our minds function, just as it is normal for us to experience difficulties with the way our bodies work. The design of our bodies is not perfect and problem free, and nor is the design of our minds. Many thinkers, such as Freud, believe that emotional suffering is part of being human.

The drawbacks of having an intelligent mind

Our brains equip us with high intelligence, the capacity for abstract thought, imagination and self-awareness. We can see into the future and make forward plans, and we can imagine limitless hypothetical scenarios. These abilities are highly advantageous, but they come with a price: we are vulnerable to psychological problems. As clinical psychologist Paul Gilbert puts it: 'Our human imagination can give rise to wonderful art, but also the most hideous of tortures.'

'Often it is just lack of imagination that keeps man from suffering very much.'

Marcel Proust

Paul Gilbert points out that new adaptations, whether in the brain or the body, come with disadvantages. For example, walking on two legs gives us the advantage of having our hands free, but means we are prone to back problems because being upright puts a strain on our spine.

He believes our new, higher-level mental capabilities often do not work well with the more ancient parts of our minds. We still have our basic emotions and urges, and these reactions in our mind are fast, automatic, powerful and difficult to control.

For example, if we are rejected, we experience the basic, automatic emotional response: sadness. But our active, intelligent, self-aware minds do not stop there. We want to find an abstract explanation for the rejection. So we use our powers of thought to ponder the case. We imagine how we appear to others: what defect do they see that makes me so undesirable? We compare our qualities to other people: am I as interesting as everybody else? We think back to the past and recall the time no one talked to us at a party. We look into the future and imagine ourselves being rejected again and again, seeing a lonely road ahead. The emotional parts of our brain respond to these imaginings with more sadness. So our self-reflective and imaginative abilities lock us into a mental cage of rumination and depression.

Another problem with our minds is they were not designed to deal with modern life – we evolved living in small groups in prehistory. We are not necessarily very well equipped, emotionally, to deal with the world today. For example, many of us live alone and do not feel part of a close-knit, cooperative group. Psychologists Baumeister and Leary point out that our brains are wired for having connections with others; we desire the emotional security of knowing we live in a network of humans who care about our existence. One fundamental human motivation is the need to belong, and this need is not easy to fulfil in today's anonymous cities.

> our minds were not designed to deal with modern life

What is 'normal' psychology and mental health?

In everyday life we tend to think in terms of normal and abnormal.

'What we call "normal" in psychology is really a psychopathology of the average, so undramatic and so widely spread that we don't even notice it ordinarily.'

Abraham Maslow, psychologist, 1908–1970

Most psychologists do not see a sharp distinction between 'normal' and 'abnormal' psychological difficulties. Issues lie on the continuum, with many of us experiencing some of the signs of psychological difficulty at some point or other in our lives.

Types of psychological problem

Different societies have different ideas about what they define as a psychological 'problem'. The American Psychiatric Association produces a classification system called the 'Diagnostic and Statistical Manual of Mental Disorders' (DSM IV) which puts our psychological difficulties into different categories, with criteria for each, so we can make the judgement as to whether someone is suffering from a particular difficulty or not.

Classification systems like this are controversial in psychology, as these systems see psychological problems in a medical way. Some problems which affect our minds are caused by recognised biological disease processes, for example, dementia. But many are not a result of any recognised underlying disease processes. Half of the problems described in the DSM IV, for example, depression, are just descriptions of patterns of behaviours and emotions that we find problematic.

Anxiety problems: the most common psychological difficulties

We all experience anxiety – it is a natural emotional response we have to help protect ourselves from danger. But some of us experience an over-activation of this response. Anxiety problems range in their triggers, severity and impact on our lives.

1 Specific phobia

A phobia is an excessive fear in reaction to certain objects or specific situations. Most of us are afraid of something, for example, about 25 per cent of us are frightened of snakes. The most common phobias are of:

- animals, including insects like wasps and bees, and also spiders
- heights
- blood, injections and injuries
- enclosed spaces
- flying.

One psychological explanation for phobias comes from behavioural psychologists such as Watson, who showed phobias can be learned through classical conditioning. For example, most dental phobics suffered a painful visit to a dentist in the past. Mild anxiety about the pain can inflate in our imaginations into strong fear when contemplating a future visit.

It is not always possible to trace the origin of phobias like this though, and some phobias are easier to acquire than others. According to Martin Seligman, we are more naturally vulnerable to developing fears of dangers from our evolutionary past, such as animals, large insects and small injuries. Despite the fact that modern inventions like traffic, cigarettes and guns are far more dangerous objectively, it is rare for people to become phobic of them.

2 Generalised anxiety

Sometimes excess anxiety is not tied to a specific situation, but is more diffuse. We all have some worries: it becomes defined as Generalised Anxiety Disorder when it goes on every day for months and is associated with signs such as:

- restlessness
- problems concentrating
- irritability
- muscle tension
- poor sleep.

In Generalised Anxiety Disorder, the worries are varied, for example, money and family concerns, health, performance at work or studies, fear of accidents, and also worry about what worry will do to us. These are the same types of worry all of us have, but become focused on unlikely events or events in the distant future. Psychologists such as Michel Dugas emphasise the role of thinking processes in this type of anxiety. For example, he proposes that we become generally anxious when we cannot tolerate uncertainty. For example, we believe it will keep us safe if we can anticipate every possible negative outcome, by thinking 'what if?' thoughts.

> we become generally anxious when we cannot tolerate uncertainty

3 Panic attacks and agoraphobia

Have you ever had or seen someone have a panic attack? A panic attack is an intense experience of fear with symptoms such as breathlessness, dizziness and trembling, becoming so alarming that people often present themselves at emergency rooms.

Some sufferers avoid situations they think might trigger a panic, such as busy public places. For these individuals, their fear of panic means they are reluctant to go out of the house, so they become agoraphobic.

Many of us might get a little alarmed from time to time about odd sensations in our bodies, such as occasional palpitations, or feelings of dizziness. But according to psychologist David Clark, when we panic, we interpret bodily sensations like this in a more extreme, catastrophic way, thinking they are a sign that we are about to faint, collapse or have a heart attack. These frightening thoughts prompt our bodies to release adrenalin, causing even more physical sensations like a pounding heart, so we become caught in a vicious cycle. Clark believes the central fear in panic attacks is the fear of losing control of our body or mind.

4 Social phobia

Social phobia can appear similar to panic – with this problem, people also get anxious in public. The main fear is we will embarrass ourselves or look anxious in social situations or when we are performing in front of others.

Almost all of us are anxious in some situations, for example, many of us would be anxious about giving a speech in front of hundreds of people. In social phobia, this kind of anxiety is more intense or problematic.

For Clark and Wells, the central problem is that in social phobia we have a negative image of the way we come across to others. We focus our attention on the things we are doing wrong, such as stumbling over words, and are harsh and self-critical. With our attention focused in this way, it becomes difficult to interact in a genuine, spontaneous way, thus giving ourselves even more reason to criticise our social performance. The fear is of what other people are thinking of us but, in reality, the critical thoughts about our performance are coming from our own minds.

5 Obsessive-compulsive disorder

With obsessive-compulsive disorder (OCD), we are also preoccupied with the thoughts generated in our own minds. In this
problem, the person experiences intrusive, upsetting thoughts
that are unwanted, and against the person's natural inclinations and nature. The thoughts are often about threatening
themes such as contamination, sex or violence. The thoughts
are extremely distressing, so a person tries to reduce distress via
actions, such as checking, handwashing or repeating a mental
ritual such as a prayer to 'neutralise' the distressing thoughts.
For example, a conscientious mother has the upsetting thought
of her child dying of an infection. So she repeats her washing
and cleaning to try and get rid of the anxiety.

Psychologists such as Paul Salkovkis see OCD as resulting from
our usual everyday thinking processes. Most of us get the occasional unpleasant thought that makes us doubt ourselves. For
example, after we leave the house we might worry we have left
the iron on, and have the momentary fear our negligence will
cause a fire. For most of us, these thoughts just cause momentary discomfort, easy to dismiss.

But for some, the intrusive thought is more upsetting, so they
attempt to suppress or neutralise it. Yet these suppression
attempts make the thought more powerful. This is because our
thoughts cannot be controlled like this. For example, try your
hardest to not think about the image of a pink giraffe for the
next ten minutes, and keep reminding yourself to suppress all
thoughts of pink giraffes. You will inevitably keep thinking of
a pink giraffe – the mental process of suppressing a thought
draws our attention to the thought.

6 Post-traumatic stress disorder

People with post-traumatic stress (PTSD) after a life-threaten-
ing incident also experience upsetting, intrusive thoughts. The
key features of PTSD are:

- experiencing memories, 'flashbacks' or dreams about the trauma
- avoiding reminders of the incident
- feeling 'over-aroused', for example, irritability, poor sleep and difficulty concentrating.

Most if not all people who go through a traumatic experience will experience some of these problems for a while. But for some people they do not go away and may get worse. Extreme events like rape, war, torture, terrorism and natural disasters can all cause PTSD, but probably the most common reason for PTSD in this country is road traffic accidents. Twenty per cent of people who have a road traffic accident will develop this difficulty. It is also fairly common after childbirth, with about 1 to 5 per cent of women reporting post-traumatic stress symptoms.

The problem for people with PTSD is that the traumatic memories do not get processed and integrated in the usual way. People are more likely to get PTSD if they feel they should have been able to control or prevent the traumatic incident, and therefore experience more guilt, shame and anger about the event. For example, women who had firm plans for a 'natural' childbirth are more traumatised by a childbirth that requires a medical intervention than those who did not have such plans.

Despite the devastating impact of PTSD, some people find that after they have recovered they experience what is called 'post-traumatic growth'. They feel the trauma made them rethink their priorities and leads to improvements in their lives such as:

- a greater appreciation of the small things
- increased confidence in their capacity to cope
- more compassion for others
- improved relationships.

brilliant example

The mystery of the disappearing penis

Different cultural believes result in different psychological problems. One of these is 'Koro', found among people in parts of Asia and Africa but hardly ever in the West. Sufferers believe their penis has been stolen or is shrinking into their bodies because of supernatural forces. They may use clamps to prevent their penis from shrinking further or get relatives to hold on to it. Women with Koro are afraid their breasts or vulva will disappear. The fear can last anything between a couple of hours to years. Koro can spread quickly in communities, causing panic and overcrowding at hospital emergency rooms.

It may be that similar problems happened in medieval Europe. In reports of witchcraft trials, women are accused of stealing people's penises using magic. Belief in the supernatural and a strong value on sexual or reproductive potency are probably important cultural factors in the development of this problem.

Eating disorders: a product of cultural factors?

Another psychological problem that is very dependent on culture is that of eating disorders. In developed societies a preoccupation with weight and controlling food intake is widespread. One study found that as many as 50 per cent of young women described themselves as having 'binges'. In a vulnerable minority of people, these difficulties spiral into anorexia or bulimia nervosa.

Anorexia is defined as the refusal to maintain normal body weight, a fear of fatness and a distorted perception of body size, seeing themselves as fat despite being emaciated. Bulimia nervosa is episodes of binge eating with attempts to get rid of the food, such as self-induced vomiting.

In both conditions sufferers place great importance on their shape and weight in evaluating their self-worth. About 80 to 90 per cent of sufferers are women, but eating disorders are thought to be becoming more common in men.

Psychiatrist Chris Fairburn says that people with eating disorders believe they will achieve a sense of control and better self-esteem from losing weight. So they set strict rules about their eating behaviour. The difference between the two problems is:

> In anorexia: people stick to these rules rigidly, so lose weight.
>
> In bulimia: people break these dietary rules, so try to compensate by vomiting.

The evidence shows that cultural factors are important in the development of these problems. When societies start to value thinness, disordered eating increases. For example, a study by Ann Becker showed the incidence of self-induced vomiting in teenage girls in Fiji went from 0 per cent to 11 per cent in just three years after the introduction of television. The girls watched programmes such as 'Beverly Hills 90210' and felt the pressure to emulate the slender body shape of the characters. One of the Fijian girls said: 'I want myself to be like that, to be that thin.'

The number one cause of disability worldwide: depression

All of us have mood swings, and most if not almost all of us go through times when we feel low, and might have a few nights of sleeping badly. Low moods are thought to be nature's way of signalling there is something wrong. But for some of us, these feelings become far more intense and problematic. Depression is defined as experiencing signs such as:

- low mood
- less interest or pleasure in almost all activities
- poor sleep, or sleeping too much
- loss of appetite and weight loss, or increased appetite and weight gain
- agitated behaviour
- difficulty in thinking or concentrating
- tiredness or loss of energy
- feelings of worthlessness or excessive guilt
- thoughts about death.

Depression is a devastating experience. Sufferer and biologist Lewis Wolpert calls it 'malignant sadness' and describes his depression as 'the worst experience of my life'. According to the World Health Organisation, depression is the number one cause of disability worldwide.

> depression is a devastating experience

brilliant example

Wealth, fame, talent and beauty are no protection from depression. Well-known people who have suffered from depression include:

Woody Allen	Agatha Christie
Princess Diana	Michael Hutchence
Abraham Lincoln	Winston Churchill
Billy Joel	Angelina Jolie
Sylvia Plath	J. K. Rowling
Mozart	Michelangelo
Mark Twain	Britney Spears

Depression is usually triggered by some kind of negative event such as illness, a problem at work or divorce. These negative events often involve some kind of loss, for example, loss of a relationship or reduction in social status. But instead of feeling transient sadness, the sufferer becomes caught in a downward spiral of depression.

Psychiatrist Aaron Beck proposes that when we are depressed, we develop a negative view of ourselves, the world and the future, and we get drawn into vicious cycles. For example, the symptoms of depression, such as lack of energy, make us withdraw from usual activity, depriving us of positive experiences and giving us more time to ruminate about negative themes, causing more depression.

Bipolar disorder

For about 1 to 2 per cent of people, periods of depression are also interspersed with extreme 'highs'. This gives bipolar disorder its popular name: 'manic depression'. Driven by feelings of euphoria, sufferers experience signs that are out of character. These may involve:

- Inflated self-esteem or 'grandiosity'
- less need for sleep
- much more talkative than usual
- racing thoughts
- distractibility, switching from one topic to another
- agitation and increased activity
- engaging in behaviours with negative consequences, such as spending lots of money, having risky sex or driving too fast.

At times, people with severe depression or bipolar disorder can become out of touch with reality and experience what is known as 'psychotic' symptoms, hallucinations and delusions, as described under 'schizophrenia' below.

Schizophrenia

Schizophrenia is not one specific problem. Instead, it is the umbrella term for people who experience a variety of problems that interfere with their daily functioning, such as:

1 Hallucinations: Perceptions that are not real, most commonly hearing voices.

2 Delusions: Beliefs that are unusual and out of keeping with the rest of society, such as the idea of being chosen for a special mission by God to save the world.

3 Disorganised speech: Speech doesn't make coherent sense, or sentences appear randomly put together like a 'word salad'.

4 Disorganised behaviour: Being unable to look after oneself and carry out the activities of daily living. Or showing emotions that are inappropriate, for example, laughing when describing a personal tragedy such as losing a child.

5 Lack of activity: appearing withdrawn and flat emotionally, lacking motivation and speaking little.

Many psychologists doubt whether it is meaningful to talk about a single condition called 'schizophrenia', given the variety of the above signs. There are many misconceptions about this condition. One of the popular myths about schizophrenia is that sufferers are dangerous, but research indicates that if people get good psychiatric treatment they are no more dangerous than anyone else – and they are, in fact, more vulnerable to being a victim of an attack. Another myth is that it is 'incurable', when in fact a quarter will recover and half significantly improve.

---

brilliant example

On being sane in insane places

Can mental health professionals reliably detect 'schizophrenia'? To test this, in 1973 psychologist David Rosenhan undertook what is now a classic study. He and seven other volunteers presented themselves at psychiatric hospitals, claiming they heard voices saying 'empty', 'hollow' and 'thud'. They were all admitted as inpatients. After admission, all the 'pseudo patients' told staff their voices had stopped. Despite showing no further 'symptoms', their ordinary behaviour, for example writing notes, was interpreted as further signs of mental disturbance.

None of the staff detected that the pseudo patients were fakes. Ironically, many of the real patients did. One of them remarked: 'You're not crazy, you're a journalist, or professor.' It was not easy for the pseudo patients to get discharged, taking an average of 19 days and as long as 52 days. They were all released with a diagnosis of schizophrenia 'in remission'.

When staff at a respected teaching and research hospital heard about these findings, they told Rosenhan that their institution could never make mistakes like this. So Rosenhan agreed to send them some pseudo patients to see if this was the case. Over a three-month period, staff identified a list of 41 patients they were very confident had been sent by Rosenhan and were not really 'ill' at all. In fact, Rosenhan had not sent any pseudo-patients to the hospital.

This study made many people very sceptical, not only about the ability of mental health professionals to correctly identify problems, but about validity of the concept of 'schizophrenia' at all.

Many believe that rather than there being a sharp distinction between people who are 'schizophrenic' and those who are not, there is a continuum whereby many people show some of these signs. Studies show many people hear voices and have eccentric beliefs but because they function well, it is never identified as an 'illness'. As many as one in ten people in the general population have experienced hearing voices.

People who are not distressed by these voices do not tend to come to the attention of mental health services. Some see their voices as a positive thing. For example, Doris Stokes saw her voices as evidence of psychic powers and found success and international fame as a medium. In contrast, people who are 'diagnosed' as schizophrenic tend to experience their voices as more malevolent, powerful and frightening.

brilliant insight

Mental health and creativity

Many thinkers have speculated about an association between mental health problems and creativity. While not all artistic people suffer from mood problems, many of them do. One study of people at a writers' workshop showed that as many as 80 per cent of them had suffered from depression.

Clinical psychologist and bipolar disorder sufferer Kay Redfield Jamison argues there is a strong link between mood problems and creativity. In particular, she believes there is a strong overlap between bipolar disorder and the 'artistic temperament'. She points out the disproportionate number of writers, artists, musicians and poets who suffer from it. These include:

Ernest Hemingway	Vincent van Gogh
William Blake	Samuel Taylor Coleridge
Lord Byron	Percy Bysshe Shelley
Mary Shelley	Robert Schumann
Frank Sinatra	Graham Greene
Ray Davies	Adam Ant
Sinead O'Connor	Kurt Cobain
Patricia Cornwell	Amy Winehouse

Jamison argues that bipolar disorder's mood swings change perceptions and so ignite creative thought. In the 'high' state of mind, musicians, artists and writers are inundated with ideas and become highly productive.

Daniel Nettle believes there may be a link between schizophrenia and creative ability. People with this condition perform well on tests of divergent thinking, such as finding different, innovative uses for objects. Nettle carried out a survey of poets, artists and mathematicians, none of whom suffered from schizophrenia, and found that they reported just as much 'schizophrenia-like' experiences as patients. Nettle speculates that schizophrenia is the price we pay for having minds that are open to unusual types of thought.

Personality disorders

Finally, there is another category of psychological problem, called the 'personality disorder'. Simply put, rather than having temporary periods of difficulty, people experience long-term problems in a number of areas of their lives.

A personality disorder is defined as experiencing difficulties from early adulthood in terms of mood, behaviour and interpersonal relationships. There are a number of different categories of this kind of problem. Probably the best known is 'borderline personality disorder', defined by the sufferer experiencing signs such as:

- frantic efforts to avoid real or imagined abandonment
- a pattern of intense but unstable personal relationships, where they idealise and then devalue others
- difficulty with their sense of their own identity, having an unstable sense of who they are
- impulsivity in areas that could be damaging to themselves, for example, binge eating, reckless driving, risky sex, overspending, substance abuse
- suicidal behaviour or threats, or self-harm such as cutting
- mood swings, irritability, anxiety
- feeling 'empty'

- anger
- short-lived psychotic symptoms, such as paranoid ideas.

Although this is defined as a long-term problem, research shows this is not quite the case. One study found 86 per cent of sufferers no longer had borderline personality disorder ten years later. People labelled as having borderline personality disorder have often experienced abuse and neglect in their childhoods. Roth and Fonagy believe that central to this problem is a disruption in parental bonding and attachment. Because of a poor relationship with care-givers, sufferers did not develop emotional security and the ability to regulate their own emotions and soothe themselves.

Why do some people suffer from emotional and psychological problems and not others?

People who have severe emotional difficulties such as borderline personality disorder are very likely to have suffered adverse or abusive childhoods. As described in Chapter 3, the way we are treated in childhood affects the way our brains develop. The connections in our brains are shaped by the amount of affection and responsive care that we do or do not receive. In her book *Why Love Matters*, Sue Gerhardt explains that inadequate parental care produces a high level of the stress hormone cortisol. This hormone inhibits the physical development of the brain in ways that leave us more vulnerable to emotional problems.

But not all children who receive inadequate care go on to develop problems. Emotional difficulties are thought to be due to a combination of biological, psychological and social factors, known as the biopsychosocial model:

1 Biological: genetic vulnerability, problems in brain development in the womb and childbirth, the physical action of neurons and neurotransmitters in our brains.

2 Psychological: events in our own minds such as our thoughts, emotions, desires, the way we make sense of our experiences, our ways of seeing the world, and our behavioural choices.

3 Social: relationships and social circumstances that impact on our minds and cause us stress, for example:

- extreme adversity such as war, repressive government regimes, political instability
- childhood adversity, such as inadequate parenting, neglect, emotional, physical and sexual abuse
- unemployment, poverty, lack of housing, living in an area of high crime
- victimisation: crime, aggression, bullying, domestic abuse
- discrimination because of race, gender, sexuality, repressive roles and devaluation of certain groups
- inequality: being in an unequal less cohesive society, with high levels of distrust and dissatisfaction that breed psychological distress
- poor work conditions, unrealistic work load, threat of redundancy
- lack of social support
- life events such as bereavement, divorce, retirement
- poor education.

We all have a certain level of vulnerability for developing problems, depending on our biological and psychological make-up. Whether or not we develop a problem depends on the amount and type of stress we are put under in our lives. This is known as the 'diathesis-stress' model, where 'diathesis' means 'predisposition'.

How to solve psychological problems

Because human problems operate at different levels, they can be tackled in different ways. They can be addressed at a societal level by preventing child abuse and inequality, for example. Biological interventions, such as antidepressant drugs, can be useful, particularly for severe depression.

Research shows that psychological therapies are effective, not just for anxiety and depression but for psychoses, too. On the whole, people who obtain therapy are more likely to recover and do so more quickly than those without therapy. But as many as two-thirds of people with psychological difficulties suffer in silence and do not seek help.

> people who obtain therapy are more likely to recover

Types of psychological interventions

There are numerous types of psychological therapy. Some have been well researched and are of proven effectiveness. What follows is only an introduction to the subject of therapy – in the Further reading and resources section there is a list of websites and organisations where you can find out more.

Some of the best known and most well established types of therapy are as follows:

1 Behavioural and cognitive-behavioural therapies

Behaviour therapy was developed by theorists such as BF Skinner, Joseph Wolpe and Hans Eysenk. It assumes psychological problems are learned, and so can be unlearned, using the principles of operant and classical conditioning. Cognitive-behavioural therapy (CBT) also uses these ideas, but includes a focus on thinking patterns as well. The originators of cognitive approaches such as Aaron Beck and Albert Ellis emphasise the importance of the role of thinking when we are distressed. Changing the way we think can help us change the way we feel. There are a huge number of schools of behaviour therapy and

CBT, which are useful for a range of difficulties including anxiety, depression and psychosis; and therapies can be delivered either individually, with groups or in families.

There are some promising newer approaches arising from this therapy tradition, such as 'Acceptance and commitment therapy' and 'compassionate mind training'.

2 Interpersonal psychotherapy

Interpersonal psychotherapy (IPT) was developed by Klerman and Weissman and works on the assumption that psychological problems are accompanied by problematic relationships or lack of satisfying relationships. The focus is on helping clients improve their relationships and social networks. IPT is very effective for a number of difficulties, in particular depression and bulimia nervosa.

3 Systemic therapies

Systemic therapies are based on the idea that difficulties are best understood, not by focusing on the 'problematic individual', but on the 'systems' people are in. We are interconnected, for example as families and communities, and a change in one person will affect another. One type of systemic therapy is 'structural' family therapy, developed by Salvador Minuchin. This focuses on improving the functioning of the whole family when an individual is identified as having a problem. Systemic approaches are helpful for children with behaviour problems, adolescents with anorexia and adults with a range of issues including depression and psychoses. More recent approaches arising from the systemic school of thinking include 'narrative' and 'solution-focused' therapy.

4 Humanistic therapies

These therapies are often referred to as 'counselling'. The approach was founded by Carl Rogers, and is based on the idea that a person in distress has experienced some conditions that have impeded their growth, in particular that they have experienced a lack of unconditional positive regard. The therapist will focus on empathy, acceptance, openness and warmth. In general there is less emphasis on techniques in this approach, but instead helpful ways of 'being with' the client. The effectiveness of these therapies has not been tested as much as some of the other therapies, but there is some evidence they are useful, particularly the variants of this approach, which incorporate more active techniques.

5 Psychoanalysis/psychodynamic therapies

Although these therapies are different in their theories and method, they both spring from Freud's ideas and assume that psychological problems are due to unconscious processes and conflicts that originate in childhood. The focus of therapy is on delving into these unconscious processes as they play out in a therapy relationship, and uncovering the person's psychological defences. In the past practitioners of these therapies were not keen to take part in research, but there is now emerging evidence that these approaches can be effective. A recent approach arising from this therapy tradition is 'mentalisation'-based therapy, which is useful for helping people with borderline personality issues.

To illustrate how these different approaches might tackle psychological problems, here is a case example:

brilliant example

Daniel is a 35-year-old ex-soldier with a wife and two sons, aged 11 and 12. He became depressed several months after he was made redundant from the army.

He had previously spent months at a time away from home, and during his periods of leave and UK assignments his wife and sons made him the centre of their lives.

Once he became a permanent member of the household this no longer applied. His wife had an active social life of her own and he often found himself on his own in the evenings. His family were no longer so willing to do things Daniel's way, for example, at weekends he liked everyone to get up early, but his wife and children preferred a lie-in. His wife and sons were untidy – in fact, the whole family regime was more lax than he liked. His wife was happy to let the boys stay up late, while he wanted them to get their sleep. Family arguments became frequent.

Daniel missed the camaraderie of his army colleagues and didn't have any friends locally. He worried about finances: his redundancy money was running out and he was struggling to find permanent work.

Daniel's mother had suffered from depression, and he had a very poor relationship with his father who was domineering and always seemed to be in a bad temper. Daniel had vowed he'd never be like that when he had kids.

As the months passed, Daniel felt less and less respected by his family, and became withdrawn and irritable. He lost respect for himself as well. He had been proud of himself as a soldier, but now he was just in a string of low-paid, temporary jobs. He became increasingly miserable, snappy and slept badly.

One day the final straw came. He overheard his wife and kids in the next room planning a day out to the local beach. He heard his younger son say, 'But do we have to take Dad?'

On hearing this, Daniel became tearful, something he hadn't done for years. He was afraid he had become just like his own dad. He felt like a failure, as a father, a husband and a man.

In brief, this is what Daniel could expect if he went for some of the different types of therapy:

Cognitive-behavioural therapy: His therapist would help him take up potentially rewarding activities, and help him reduce his avoidance of his family. Together they would address his negative thoughts that he was a 'failure'.

Systemic therapy: Daniel would be invited to bring members of his family to his appointment. The therapist would probably have a co-therapist behind a one-way screen, to help address the patterns of interactions and roles that are contributing to the issues.

Humanistic therapy: Daniel's counsellor would help him explore and express his emotions, and reflect back understanding, acceptance and unconditional positive regard, to assist Daniel in finding his own way through his difficulties.

Psychodynamic therapy: The therapist may be looking for unconscious conflicts in relation to Daniel's feelings about his father, and make interpretations about the way these are playing out in his life.

Interpersonal psychotherapy: Daniel opted to undertake interpersonal psychotherapy. He and the therapist concluded that the central problem was that he was having difficulty in coping with the transition from the role of soldier and part-time dad, to civilian life and full-time family life. This new role involved losses and changes in his relationships and meant his needs were not being met. The old relationships, which gave him his identity, sense of belonging, purpose and self-esteem, were all tied up with the army. He was no longer the 'returning hero' and head of the family; his new relationships were as an ordinary dad and a full-time husband. Daniel recognised he was inadvertently repeating the pattern of his own father's parenting style. He was behaving in an authoritarian style, expressing his needs angrily, and withdrawing when he did not get the reaction he wanted.

Daniel needed to mourn and let go of his old life and role. He needed to recognise his new role in the family and negotiate this with his wife and sons. He learned to express his views in a way that was more likely to get a positive response from his family, and to negotiate rather than dictate. He started sharing the responsibility for finances with his wife and this relieved his stress levels. Daniel began developing a new social network: playing football regularly and making some new friends. He and his wife started socialising as a couple. He started feeling better. He continued to struggle to find permanent work, but because his home life was much improved, he was able to cope with it.

Although therapies have different techniques and theories, they are often similarly effective, and it may be that Daniel would have benefited from any of the above approaches. Having a good therapist who is enthusiastic about their model, a good client–therapist relationship, and a client who is willing to invest in the therapy are probably just as important as the type of therapy itself.

What to do if you or a close friend or family member has psychological problems

If you think you might be experiencing some of the above or other psychological problems, then a good first step is to talk over your concerns with someone you trust. If you decide to seek further help, make an appointment with your GP who should be able to help you decide whether further help is appropriate. They should be able to discuss options for therapeutic input, medication or consultation with a specialist team.

> a good first step is to talk over your concerns with someone you trust

There are also self-help books and websites for all of the psychological problems discussed here. Research shows that a self-help approach can be effective, specifically, self-help using CBT approaches for anxiety problems and mild to moderate depression. Peer support and voluntary organisations can be helpful for a wide range of difficulties. For details of some of these, see the Further reading and resources section.

Many aspects of modern life and our own human nature can make us unhappy. But what about the flip side to this? What makes us happy? This is explored in the final chapter.

brilliant recap

- We have new, high-level intellectual abilities intertwined with ancient social and emotional needs – these, combined with the challenges of our modern, unnatural lives, leave us vulnerable to emotional suffering.

- There is no sharp distinction between 'normal' and 'abnormal' psychological problems, rather the severity of these lies on a continuum.

- Love and appropriate care in childhood matters for future psychological health.

- Psychological problems are a result of the interplay of biological, psychological and social factors.

- Psychological therapy is an effective way of addressing problems.

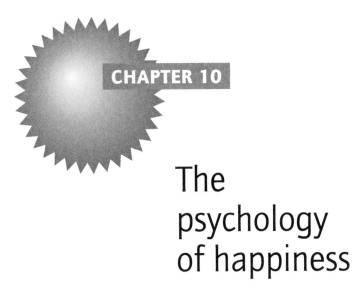

CHAPTER 10

The psychology of happiness

Overcoming psychological problems like anxiety and depression will improve our well-being. But even without psychological problems like these, some people are happier than others. What is happiness and how can we achieve it?

Early psychologist William James thought this was an important question, but during the behaviourist years psychology largely ignored fuzzy concepts like happiness. When emotion became a respectable area of study, psychologists tended to look at human suffering instead. Perhaps surprisingly, human happiness has only become a big topic in psychology in the last 15 years or so.

Why happiness is important

Happiness is not just a good thing in itself, but it has all sorts of other benefits for us and others. It makes us nicer to be around: when we are happier we are more even-tempered. Happiness does not make us more selfish, as some people think, instead research shows it makes us more kind and generous.

Happiness may even be associated with living longer – a well-known study of the life expectancy of a group of nuns in America revealed a link between positive emotion and longevity. The ones who had expressed more positive emotions in samples of their writing from the 1930s lived on average ten years longer. Whether positive emotions are the cause of a long life or this is just a correlation is unknown, but the researchers in this study suggested that happiness might be as important for our long-term health as giving up smoking.

What is 'happiness' anyway?

Academics like to define something before they investigate it. But happiness is a difficult concept to pin down, as shown by the fact that psychologists struggle to agree on a definition. Psychologists tend to use different terms for it such as 'well-being' and 'life satisfaction'. But most definitions include at least two aspects. One aspect is experiencing positive feelings: joy, elation, laughter and physical pleasure. The other part is your overall judgement of your life satisfaction, a more cognitive component.

Psychologist Sonja Lyubomirsky sees happiness as 'the experience of joy, contentment or positive well-being, combined with a sense that one's life is good, meaningful and worthwhile'.

How happy are you?

Researchers measure happiness with simple questionnaires. Try the 'Satisfaction with Life' scale, constructed by Ed Diener and his colleagues. Give yourself a score for each of the five items according to how much you agree or disagree with the statements.

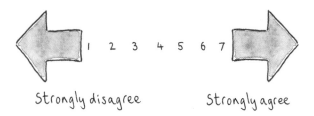

1   In most ways my life is close to my ideal.

2   The conditions of my life are excellent.

3   I am satisfied with my life.

4   So far I have got the important things I want in life.

5   If I could live my life over, I would change almost nothing.

Add up your scores and see where you fit:

31–35	Extremely satisfied
26–30	Satisfied
21–25	Slightly satisfied
20	Neutral
15–19	Slightly dissatisfied
10–14	Dissatisfied
5–9	Extremely dissatisfied

Your scores on questionnaires like this are sensitive to momentary fluctuations in your emotional state. The kind of mood you are in at the moment, positive or gloomy, will have a big effect on your satisfaction rating. Researchers have found a transient good mood caused by finding a coin in a vending machine can be enough to make people rate their whole lives as better. You could try rating yourself on different occasions and averaging your scores to get a more representative overall picture.

What does and doesn't determine happiness?

What do you think makes a difference to human happiness? How important do you think these five things are for your overall happiness levels?

1   Good looks

2   Living in a sunny climate

3   Having children

4 Youthfulness

5 Wealth

Research suggested that these five matter very little, or even not at all.

1 Good looks

Some studies show a link between good looks and happiness. People who see themselves as good looking also rate themselves as happier. But when psychologist Ed Diener used objective ratings of people's looks, the link disappeared. This suggests it is the *belief* that you are good looking that goes along with happiness, rather than the good looks themselves.

2 Living in a sunny climate

Although people in cold and rainy climates, shivering under an umbrella, imagine that people in sunny places are happier, this is not true. People in California are no happier than people in the Midwestern states. In the UK, people in the extreme northerly areas such as the Orkney and Shetland Islands and the Outer Hebrides seem to have the greatest level of well-being. And some of the happiest countries have relatively less sunshine, for example, Sweden and Denmark.

3 Children

We feel children should make us happy – it is a belief deeply ingrained in our culture. But although many parents insist their children are a great source of joy, research suggests otherwise. There is little evidence that having kids makes us happier – if anything it is the opposite. Having several children is associated with less life satisfaction, and surveys show that parents rate looking after children as less enjoyable than housework.

4 Youthfulness

We often associate youth with good times and old age with infirmity. However, age does not seem to have a big effect on happiness. In old age we continue to enjoy the same level of emotional well-being as younger people. Psychologists Laura Carstensen and Susan Turk Charles even suggest that older people may even be happier. Their research shows older people experience more positive emotions and fewer negative ones. They believe this is because older people prioritise better and spend more time on activities they know they will genuinely enjoy, rather than trying everything out in the way younger people do. Carstensen and Charles discovered older people are better at managing negative feelings, for example, older people become less angry during disagreements with their spouse.

5 Wealth

As you would suspect, having enough money for your basic needs is a necessary condition for happiness. People who do not have enough money to pay for food, shelter and clothing are much less happy, in all countries. But once a country has reached a modest level of wealth, the happiness of the population does not increase when it becomes even richer. Economist Richard Layard observes that people in developed countries are no happier now than they were 50 years ago. For example, between 1970 and 1990 the average income in the USA increased by 300 per cent, but happiness ratings did not increase.

Why are we no happier even though we are objectively richer?

According to Nobel Prize-winning psychologist Daniel Kahneman, the answer lies in the way you reply to this question. Which would you prefer:

Earning £100,000 a year, but everyone else around you
earning £150,000

or:

Earning £90,000 and everyone else around you earning
£70,000.

Most people say they would prefer the second. We would
rather earn less, but be doing better in comparison with everyone else.

Kahneman concludes that once we have got enough to live on,
the amount of money we have only matters in relation to everyone else's level of wealth. So greater riches do not make us
happier when other people around us have become richer as well.

Psychologist Tim Kasser goes further and believes that material values breed dissatisfaction and anxiety. He says a focus on
accumulating wealth undermines our relationships, lowers our
self-esteem and is associated with feelings of insecurity.

Why do we crave more money even though it doesn't make us happier?

Surveys show that when you ask people what would make them
happier, most people say 'more money'. Why is this, when it
doesn't? The answer may be that although human beings cooperate with one another, they are also in competition with each
other. In nature, when the competition is doing better than you
it poses a serious threat to your survival and you need to take
steps to address it. Just as trees in the forest need to grow tall if
they have tall neighbours, so we feel the need to keep up with
the Joneses.

Our competitive human nature makes us want things. But a
reason we are not satisfied with more money is because we may
be confusing 'wanting' with 'liking'. Psychologist Daniel Nettle

says we often want the things we do not necessarily like very much. He proposes that these two feelings are controlled by two different brain systems, with different neurotransmitters. We assume that when we experience a strong want, we will like it when we get it. But just because you desperately want something does not mean you will get much pleasure from it. Daniel Gilbert calls this 'miswanting': wanting something that will not give you much enjoyment when you get it.

Although an increase of money will give you a happiness boost for a short while, you will quickly adapt to it. Brickman and Campbell call this the 'hedonic treadmill', the tendency for some pleasures to fade, and for the need for new or greater positive stimuli to replace them.

The happiness we get from buying things which are mainly about prestige, showing to ourselves and others that we are doing better than the competition, fades quickly. But not all pleasures fade fast. Research shows that people enjoy activities, such as having dinner with friends or going on holiday, more than acquiring possessions, such as a new watch or car. Happiness researchers say that to get more value from our money in terms of increased well-being, we should spend it on 'doing, not having'.

So what does make people happy?

Here are six factors that do have an impact on our well-being:

1 Economic equality

Richard Layard, among others, points out that people in societies with a more equal distribution of wealth are happier. Life satisfaction is relative: big disparities between rich and poor make the poorer people unhappier, while not making the rich any happier.

Assuming that society is not going to become economically equal any time soon, psychologist Sonja Lyubomirsky says that to be happier, we should try to avoid making social comparisons. As she puts it: 'The happier the person, the less attention she pays to how others around her are doing.' She suggests we should be alert to our tendency to make upward comparisons, and to stop our train of thought and distract ourselves with something else.

we should try to avoid making social comparisons

2 Having control

The feeling that you have the power of choice is related to well-being. For example, research suggests that if you are relatively poor but feel in control of your life, you will be happier than a rich person who does not feel in control of their life.

3 Relationships

Our relationships are probably the most significant factors in determining our happiness. Having a close, confiding relationship is important for our well-being. For many people this is their spouse, but it can also be another relative or close friend.

Making a romantic commitment makes us happier – at least for a time. Studies show that the recently married are happier for a couple of years, then they revert to their previous level of well-being. As you might expect, divorce, separation or bereavement has a negative effect on our life satisfaction.

As we are a social animal, other people are the source of many of our positive emotions. Humour, contentment, pride, pleasure, amusement, satisfaction and excitement are generated in social interactions. People can also bolster our happiness in difficult times, by providing practical and emotional support.

It is not just close friendships that matter – it also helps to have connections with the wider community. Having a sense of connection to others around you, and a role where you live, is associated with greater happiness.

4 Rewarding work

For many this sense of connection comes through work. Being in work contributes to well-being and, unsurprisingly, being unemployed is a big source of unhappiness. But research indicates that not all jobs are conducive to happiness, such as those with restrictive, poor conditions and no job security.

5 Good health in ourselves and our loved ones

Luckily for us, just as we can adapt to the pleasures in life, we can also adapt to some of its pains. We have a very good ability to adapt to ill health – for example, many people who become disabled are able to recover their previous level of happiness. However, long-term illness that interferes with our capacity to work or inflicts chronic pain makes us less happy. And if we are a full-time carer for a relative who is severely disabled and very dependent, this greatly reduces our life satisfaction.

6 A trustworthy community

If you live in a community where you can trust people, you are likely to be more contented. For example, in Norway, where people are generally very happy, one study showed that 64 per cent of people agree to the statement: 'Yes, people can be trusted.' In Brazil, where people are less happy, only 5 per cent said people can be trusted.

It is not just that happiness leads to the feeling people can be trusted. Researchers tested this by leaving wallets in public places, and counting the number that were returned. The number of wallets returned in different countries corresponded highly with people's views of their communities' trustworthiness.

The range of happiness around the world

Which countries do you think are the most happy? Which the least?

Surveys have been carried out to answer this question. On a rating scale of 1 to 10, where 1 is a low satisfaction score and 10 high, here are some examples of average life satisfaction:

Switzerland	8.38	China	7.05
Denmark	8.16	France	6.76
Sweden	8.02	Japan	6.53
Ireland	7.87	Nigeria	6.40
USA	7.71	India	6.21
UK	7.48	Russia	5.37
Italy	7.24	Bulgaria	5.03
Spain	7.13		

Most people report above average happiness in the UK, describing themselves as moderately or very happy. The most frequent rating is 8 out of 10. Although the majority are contented enough, very few people say they are a 10, and most people have a 'happiness gap' between their level of happiness now and where they feel they could be.

How we can we become happier?

One of the first psychologists who focused on understanding how we become happy was Abraham Maslow. He constructed his well-known 'hierarchy of needs' in 1954. His idea was that we all have a set of basic needs, and when these are met we try to fulfil the ones at the next level. The needs are:

- basic biological needs such as hunger and thirst
- the need for safety and security
- the need for love and a sense of belonging
- self-esteem and recognition
- need for knowledge and understanding
- aesthetic needs, such as order and beauty
- need for self-actualisation – fulfilling your personal potential.

Once you have your more basic needs met, according to Maslow, you can 'self actualise'. Self-actualised people are those who have 'become everything that one is capable of becoming'. People who are self-actualised are more satisfied, enjoy life more and are happier. Although his thinking has been influential, Maslow did not carry out much actual research on these ideas.

Psychologist Michael Argyle was among the first to conduct systematic research on how we become happy. He concluded that people need a close relationship with someone, a network of friends, a job that is at just the right level of challenge and an absorbing leisure interest.

The development of 'positive psychology'

In 1998, the question 'how can we become happier?' became a big topic of investigation, when Martin Seligman founded 'positive psychology', the study of well-being and human flourishing. Seligman received a cheque for 1.5 million dollars from an anonymous benefactor to start this branch of psychology, later discovering the donor was billionaire philanthropist Charles Feeney. Positive psychology is now hugely successful, attracting lots of funding and media attention.

Martin Seligman believes there are five aspects to well-being:

1 Positive emotions: feeling good and being satisfied with your life.

2 Engagement: the sense of being completely absorbed in something in the moment, known as the state of 'flow'.

3 Relationships: most good things happen in the context of relationships. As Seligman puts it, 'Very little that is positive is solitary'.

4 Meaning: having the sense that your life is about something bigger than yourself, such as caring for people, discovering truth, or building something worthwhile.

5 Accomplishment: having something you pursue or want to master for its own sake, which does not need to have great meaning; for example, Martin Seligman likes playing bridge.

Seligman calls these five the 'PERMA' theory, and in his view well-being is more than just experiencing positive emotions and feeling good; instead this is only one of the components. He believes that practical steps to happiness should be built around these five aspects.

What is your positivity ratio?

Psychologist Barbara Fredrickson, on the other hand, emphasises good feelings in her view of happiness. Her idea is that well-being is a result of having more positive emotion in our lives than negative: to be happy we need to experience at least three happy emotions for every unhappy one.

> positive emotions have an 'undoing' effect on negative ones

She has discovered through her research that positive emotions have an 'undoing' effect on negative ones. She found people recover more quickly from giving a presentation in stressful circumstances when they watch an uplifting film clip afterwards, such as seeing a small dog playing with a flower.

According to Fredrickson, positive emotions cause the 'broaden and build' effect, whereby happiness makes us more creative, open, resilient and willing to try new things.

She says that in reality most of us only experience a two to one ratio of positive emotion to negative, falling short of the three to one level we really need to flourish. To test your positivity ratio go to: http://www.positivityratio.com/single.php

Born to be happy?

Other psychologists emphasise the importance of our genetic predisposition for happiness. There seems to be a strong inherited component. Identical twins are very likely to have a similar level of happiness, even if they grew up in different families. The heritability of happiness is estimated to be about 50 per cent.

According to Daniel Nettle, the best predictor of a person's happiness in the future is how happy they are now. People report similar levels of happiness at different points of time, such as seven or twelve years apart, even though their circumstances may have changed. So we have a 'set point', a basic level of happiness.

The happiness formula

If our biology determines half of our happiness, what about the other half? Sonja Lyubomirsky believes only about 10 per cent of our happiness is determined by our circumstances, such as our marital status, income and health. In her view, if you waved a magic wand and changed these to your ideal, at most you would only become 10 per cent happier.

According to Lyubomirsky, the remaining 40 per cent of factors that determine happiness are our intentional activities. These include how we choose to spend our leisure time, how we relate to our family and friends, our personal goals, how we make sense of the world, how we look after our bodies and how we behave when confronted with a problem.

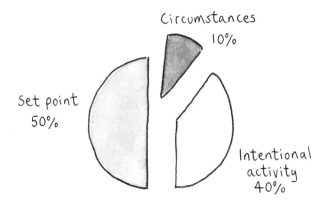

Source: Lyubomirsky, S. (2010). Reprinted with kind permission of the author.

Happiness equals your inherited 'set point', plus the conditions of your life, plus your voluntary activities.

The opportunity: the 40 per cent you can change

If this is right, what practical measures can you take to improve your happiness? You cannot change your biological predisposition. You cannot easily change your circumstances such as marital status, income and health.

But you can change the 40 per cent that is 'intentional activity'. These voluntary things are largely under your control: they are what we do. So as an individual we can take practical steps to increasing our happiness.

'Happiness is not something readymade. It comes from your own actions.'

Dalai Lama

Psychological research suggests there are a number of strategies you could use to increase your well-being. Not all of them will work for you: Lyubomirsky cautions that we should take into account our individuality. Some of the following strategies for happiness will strike a chord with you; other approaches will connect less well with you.

Here are five practical ways to think about how you could improve your future happiness:

1 Do enjoyable, satisfying things

A simple but effective way of increasing well-being is to do more of the things that give you positive feelings. What kind of activities make you feel excitement, sensory pleasure, contentment, humour, satisfaction or pride? Research shows that when we arrange more enjoyable activities for ourselves, our happiness rating increases. It may sound obvious, but so many of us get caught up with other pressures in life that we do not prioritise doing the things we genuinely enjoy.

According to Michael Argyle, the things that give people the most pleasure are socialising, sex, success/achievement, physical activity, sport, nature, food, music, reading and alcohol. The top rated activities for enjoyment are eating with friends and sex.

2 Have goals

But just transitory pleasure is not enough for most people. Lyubomirsky says: 'Find a happy person and you will find a project.' An important part of well-being for many is the feeling they are working towards something. Your goal needs to be meaningful to you and involve activity you find rewarding for its own sake.

3 Find flow

Psychologist Mihaly Csikszentmihaliya says we are at our happiest when we are engaged in something that is so absorbing we forget ourselves and have a sense of time flying. Activities where you find 'flow' need to engage your attention fully and be challenging at a level that suits your ability. Feeling 'in the zone' can happen in a wide variety of pursuits such as sports, games, music, art or work.

4 Exercise

Most of us will get a happiness boost from exercise. People who exercise at least three times a week for half an hour are happier, and those who take up exercise experience an increase in their well-being. Lyubomirsky says it is the most immediate way to lift mood. She goes as far as to guarantee that regular exercise will make you happier.

> regular exercise will make you happier

Exercise gives us a sense of mastery, takes our mind away from worries, and increases our self-esteem. If you have not done this already, your happiness should increase if you find an exercise you enjoy that fits into your lifestyle.

5 Use your strengths

Martin Seligman suggests that choosing activities that play to your strengths will give you more satisfaction and make you more likely to find 'flow'. He and Christopher Peterson have developed a list of human strengths, a classification system which is a kind of antidote to the Diagnostic and Statistical Manual of Mental Disorders, the catalogue of our problems. According to Peterson and Seligman, human beings have six overarching virtues, consisting of 24 strengths. These are:

Wisdom and knowledge

1 Curiosity: being interested in the world

2 Love of learning

3 Judgement: the ability to think critically while being open-minded

4 Ingenuity: creativity and ability to do things in novel ways

5 Social/emotional intelligence

6 Perspective: the ability to see the world in a wise and mature way

Courage

7 Valour: bravery, when facing physical or psychological threats

8 Perseverance

9 Integrity, genuineness and honesty

Humanity and love

10 Kindness and generosity

11 Loving and allowing oneself to be loved

Justice

12 Citizenship, duty, teamwork and loyalty

13 Fairness and equity

14 Leadership

Temperance

15 Self control

16 Prudence, discretion and caution

17 Humility and modesty

Transcendence

18 Appreciation of beauty and excellence

19 Gratitude

20 Hope/optimism

21   Spirituality, sense of purpose, faith and religiousness

22   Forgiveness and mercy

23   Playfulness and humour

24   Zest, passion, enthusiasm

To help you find your strengths, there is a free online questionnaire called the VIA, the 'Values In Action' Inventory of Strengths at: www.authentichappiness.org

The result of this questionnaire should show your 'signature' strengths. These are the aspects of you that make you think: 'Yes, that is the real me,' and you feel excited and motivated when using this strength.

Seligman recommends we identify our top five strengths and find new ways of using them. So if justice is one of your strengths, find a new way of expressing this, such as campaigning with a group for a cause you care about. If you have a strong appreciation of beauty, for example, the beauty in the natural world, then have plants and flowers in your home, watch nature programmes on TV and plan regular trips to the countryside.

'Seek out that particular mental attribute which makes you feel most deeply and vitally alive, along with which comes the inner voice that says 'This is the real me', and when you have found that attitude, follow it.'

William James, psychologist, 1842–1910

Savouring the moment

One feature of life is that we are so absorbed in carrying our our daily routine automatically, with our attentions elsewhere, that we fail to notice the moment. For example, we swallow our lunch quickly, barely noticing the taste, so focused are we on our plans for the afternoon. Research shows that people who take time to savour at least two pleasurable experiences a day show an increase in happiness.

What small things do you really enjoy? A strategy to try is to deliberately savour the small pleasures of the day, whatever these might be: coffee and conversation, food, looking at the sky, autumn leaves, a flock of birds, or the warmth and comfort of your bed.

'The art of being happy lies in the power of extracting happiness from common things.'

Henry Ward Beecher, clergyman and
social reformer, 1813–1887

Mindfulness meditation

Meditation is one way to increase our ability to savour the moment. Buddhists have used meditation for 2,000 years, and modern scientific research shows regular mindfulness meditation boosts well-being, reduces stress and even improves immune functioning.

Mindfulness meditation involves focusing your awareness, and when people practise this regularly they develop a different relationship with their own minds. Instead of being pulled along in our stream of consciousness, where our attention flicks from topic to topic, we develop a sense of being able to step aside from this, and to notice mental events as just mental events, things that pass through our minds. This makes us less vulnerable to being drawn into the downward spiral of worry and pessimistic thinking.

If you are interested in this, there may be a mindfulness meditation course offered locally. They are sometimes free when offered by Buddhist organisations. Alternatively, you can practise at home with a CD such as 'Mindfulness for Beginners' by Jon Kabat-Zinn.

brilliant tip

How to take action

A problem with these strategies for happiness is we can read about them, have good intentions, but never get round to doing them. When we resolve on a new course of action, we often fail to follow it through. Many of our good intentions in life do not translate into action, and this is known as the 'intention-behaviour gap'.

There is a simple, but effective way of bridging this gap. Research by psychologist Peter Gollwitzer shows that if we form a specific plan in our minds, we are much more likely to carry out the behaviour. This is called an 'implementation intention'.

So, for example, as well as having the general idea 'I'll do more exercise' you need to make a specific plan, such as 'I will go for a walk in the park tonight after dinner'. Gollwitzer calls this the 'strong effect of simple plans'. The reason it works is our automatic processes take over our behaviour. After dinner you are more likely to automatically walk out of the door, already knowing an intended route and length, without having to first think, plan and make a decision.

Getting more people into your daily life

If you are not experiencing enough enjoyable or satisfying inter-actions with others, your well-being will be affected. If this is true for you, one way to increase your happiness is to spend more time with your friends and loved ones.

Do you feel you don't have a good network of friends in your life at the moment? Then prioritise the making of connections, for example, by extending invitations or organising get-togethers. Unsurprisingly, research shows that people with busy social lives frequently initiate and organise social activities. If you are not meeting like-minded people naturally, then you will need to be proactive in seeking them out, for example by joining a reading group, football team, church group or by volunteering.

Make yourself happier by making other people happy

Martin Seligman concludes: 'People who care more about others are happier than those who care more about themselves.' He argues that to increase our happiness, we need to form the habit of thinking about others.

There is a great deal of research to back this up. One study showed that people who gave a small sum of money away were happier than those who spent it on themselves. Psychologist Jonathan Haidt discovered that people who did a random act of kindness once a week experienced a long-lasting boost in mood. He says doing good provides a feeling of 'elevation', a positive moral emotion, accompanied by a tingling in the skin and sense of expansion in the chest. Helping others may be better for our happiness than getting help ourselves. In one study, volunteers with multiple sclerosis who supported other sufferers actually seemed to benefit more, gaining seven times more life satisfaction than the people they were helping.

> helping others may be better for our happiness than getting help ourselves

However, this happiness activity would not suit everybody, for example, if you are already doing too much for others and becoming unhappy as a result.

Lyubomirsky says that the optimum way to boost your happiness level through altruism is to do five acts of kindness on one day of the week. Examples she gives include donating blood, helping a friend with homework, visiting an elderly relative or writing a thank-you letter. To keep the acts meaningful, you need to vary them as doing the same thing becomes routine.

Why does this make us happy? One reason is helping makes us feel connected to others. It boosts our self-esteem because we feel like a valuable social being. Helping others also brings positive consequences, such as appreciation, compliments and the likelihood that someone will do good things for us in return.

The attitude of gratitude

Happy people tend to be more grateful for the good things in their lives. Cultivating this attitude could give your well-being a boost. Noting down up to five things you are thankful for gives you a lift in mood, according to research by Lyubomirsky.

Showing your gratitude to others is happiness-enhancing, too. Jonathan Haidt asked people to write a 300-word thank-you letter to a person who had helped them in the past. They arranged a visit, then read the letter out. This exercise, although initially awkward, made people feel happy all day and sometimes into the next.

About once a week, think of three to five things you are grateful or thankful for and write them down. When people have helped you, take time to show or express your gratitude.

Be optimistic

Research confirms what we might suspect: people who have an optimistic outlook cope better with adversity and have better well-being. Optimism is about cultivating a mindset whereby we see the best in difficult situations and have positive expectations for the future.

This is not the same as 'positive thinking'. Just repeating a positive thought like a mantra does not work, and if anything the research indicates it will make you even less happy.

One way to try to cultivate optimism is to focus more frequently on the good things – deliberately pay more attention to the positive aspects of your life. As William James put it: 'My experience is what I agree to attend to.'

⊿ exercise   Boosting your optimism

Try this exercise to increase your optimism: for the next week, take ten minutes before bedtime to reflect on your day and write or think about three things that went well and why.

Another exercise, devised by Laura King, is designed to increase your optimism about the future. Over the next four days, write for 20 minutes about a future you – when all your best hopes have been realised and you have met your major goals. Keep the vision realistic, rather than a fantasy like winning the lottery. Write about your future life in detail, including all aspects. For example, if your hopes are to move to the country and get a dog, learn to play the guitar, overcome your shyness, get married and work as a chef, write about what this would look and feel like on a typical day. What would the future you be doing and feeling?

Research has shown that people who wrote about their best possible selves felt a happiness boost straight away, were happier a few weeks later and had fewer health problems months afterwards.

The tyranny of positive thinking

Writer and social critic Barbara Ehrenreich believes the idea of thinking 'positively' has gone much too far. When she was diagnosed with breast cancer she was shocked to find she was told repeatedly that she had to 'be positive' and then she would beat the disease, and even to embrace the illness as a 'gift'. There is no evidence that 'positive thinking' is a cure for cancer. Ehrenreich points out that this unrealistic optimism puts a cruel burden on patients, giving them the responsibility for curing themselves and the blame if they don't.

In her book *Smile or Die: How Positive Thinking Fooled America and the World*, she argues that the destructive effect of positive thinking even played a part in the financial crisis. Gripped by unrealistic optimism, banks lent money to people who could not pay it back. Financiers who urged for more caution were sacked for their 'negativity'. Ehrenreich criticises Martin Seligman and positive psychology for adding to the popular perception that 'positive' thinking is a panacea for everything from failure, to poverty, to cancer and even death.

Your 'five a day'

Whether or not positive thinking has gone too far, there is no doubt there are things we can do for ourselves to improve our mood. A government report recommended that, just as we should try to have five fruits or vegetables a day, we should have a 'five a day approach to our psychological well-being'. So every day we should:

1 Connect: interact positively with others, share a joke with colleagues, call friends, have coffee with someone new at work or arrange social events.

2 Be active: do something that gets you moving – walking, playing active games with your children, football, gardening or jogging.

3 Give: do a favour for a friend. Give a compliment to someone, or thank them. Help out someone you do not know very well. Send an unexpected gift or card to a family member.

4 Take notice: be aware in the moment. Savour the small things of everyday life: having lunch, appreciating the beauty of the world around you.

5 Keep learning: satisfaction and interest come with learning something new. Find opportunities to gain a new skill: playing music, car maintenance, Indian cookery, wine tasting or writing.

For more ideas on how to increase your happiness, have a look at: www.actionforhappiness.org

Finding the meaning in your life

Martin Seligman and many other thinkers believe finding meaning in our lives is one of the components of well-being. If we can find an overarching purpose in our activities, we are happier. For example, a study of hospital cleaners found those who considered their role important in the larger goal of contributing to patient health were more satisfied in their jobs than those who saw their work as lacking in significance.

> if we can find an overarching purpose in our activities, we are happier

Psychiatrist Viktor Frankl is one of the most well-known writers on the importance of meaning. He was incarcerated for three years in concentration camps, including Auschwitz. His mother, father, brother and his wife perished in the camps, but despite living in the worst imaginable circumstances, he managed to find a meaning to his existence. He found it in contemplating his past, in the love he had known. Frankl believed that, as Friedrich Nietzsche put it: 'He who has a why to live can bear almost any how.'

For many, a sense of meaning comes from their spiritual beliefs. For atheists like Richard Dawkins, there is profound meaning in contemplating the beauty of the universe and the quest to unravel its mysteries. Others find it in trying to make the world a better place for people or animals, or in preserving the environment. As social beings, many of us find meaning in our friendships and family. Or we find it in our work, passions and personal goals.

What is it for you? If you are experiencing a lack of meaning, just pondering over the question, 'What is the meaning in my life?' may not be the best way of finding it. This may lead to the kind of over-thinking and rumination which is not conducive to happiness. It might be a better strategy to talk about meaning in your life with someone wise who knows you well.

But according to positive psychology, if we go down the path of deliberately doing more of the things we love, committing to our goals, using our strengths and connecting with and helping others, we should discover meaning along the way.

brilliant recap

- Once we have achieved a certain level of wealth, more money does not bring more happiness.

- Conditions in society have a significant effect on our happiness.

- There is a biological basis for our basic level of happiness.

- Happiness can be achieved despite a variety of different life circumstances.

- Good relationships and connecting with others is one of the most important aspects of well-being.

- We can increase our happiness level by changing our activities.

# Afterword

This text has only touched on some of the insights into the human mind revealed by modern psychology. The science of mental life has a long way to go – there are still many unknowns.

As we are living in a rapidly changing world, the way we behave is changing, and today's psychological findings might not be true tomorrow.

Our recent inventions – the computer, the internet and digital communication – are transforming our lives, expanding our abilities to process information and share it with each other, endowing our minds with even more power. This revolution, the Information Age, is going to have far-reaching effects on the way we think, feel and relate to each other.

But despite changes ahead, the biological blueprint for our mind has not changed for 200,000 years. We still have our basic human nature. Our minds are wired to connect with other humans; our needs as social animals will stay the same. We would all be much happier if we could organise ourselves, as a society, in a way that takes account of our needs, based on an accurate psychological appreciation of how we flourish best.

We will have to make big changes in our behaviour if we are to rise to the challenges and threats of the future: looking after the environment, improving our health, promoting equality and preventing violence and war.

If we are to achieve these we will need to advance and apply our knowledge of human psychology. The well-being of our species – and perhaps even our future survival at all – depends on us developing a better understanding of ourselves.

Further reading, resources and key references

Further reading and resources

The latest editions of works are cited where possible.

Chapter 1

Goleman, D. (2007) *Social Intelligence: The New Science of Human Relationships*. Arrow.

Kahneman, D. (2011) *Thinking, Fast and Slow*. Penguin.

Pinker, S. (1995) *The Language Instinct*. Penguin.

Pinker, S. (1999) *How the Mind Works*. Penguin.

Chapter 2

Damasio, A. (2000) *The Feeling of What Happens: Body and Emotion in the Making of Consciousness*. Vintage.

Ekman, P. (2004) *Emotions Revealed*. Phoenix.

Goleman, D. (2009) *Emotional Intelligence: Why It Can Matter More than IQ*. Bloomsbury.

Chapter 3

Cohen, D. (2012) *How the Child's Mind Develops*. Routledge.

Gerhardt, S. (2004) *Why Love Matters: How Affection Shapes a Baby's Brain*. Routledge.

Chapter 4

Nettle, D. (2009) *Personality: What Makes You the Way You Are.* Oxford University Press.

Reiss, S. (2002) *Who Am I? The 16 Basic Desires that Motivate Our Actions and Define Our Personality.* Jeremy P. Tarcher.

Chapter 5

Dunbar, R. (2010) *How Many Friends Does One Person Need? Dunbar's Number and Other Evolutionary Quirks.* Faber and Faber.

Haidt, J. (2012) *The Righteous Mind: Why Good People are Divided by Politics and Religion.* Pantheon.

Yeung, R. (2011) *I is for Influence, the New Science of Persuasion.* MacMillan.

Chapter 6

Ekman, P. (2009) *Telling Lies: Clues to Deceit in the Marketplace, Politics and Marriage.* W.W. Norton and Co.

Pinker, S. (2012) *The Better Angels of Our Nature: Why Violence has Declined.* Penguin.

Zimbardo, P. (2008) *The Lucifer Effect: How Good People Turn Evil.* Rider.

Chapter 7

Baron-Cohen, S. (2012) *The Essential Difference: Men, Women and the Extreme Male Brain.* Penguin.

Fine, C. (2011) *Delusions of Gender: The Real Science Behind the Sex Differences.* Icon Books Ltd.

Gottman, J. (2007) *The Seven Principles For Making Marriage Work.* Orion.

Chapter 8

Ariely, D. (2009) *Predictably Irrational: The Hidden Forces That Shape Our Decisions.* HarperCollins.

Fine, C. (2007) *A Mind of its Own: How your Brain Distorts and Deceives.* Icon Books Ltd.

Gilbert, D. (2007) *Stumbling on Happiness.* Harper Perennial.

Thaler, R. H. and Sunstein, C. R. (2009) *Nudge: Improving Decisions about Health, Wealth and Happiness.* Penguin.

Chapter 9

www.iapt.nhs.uk

Increasing Access to Psychological Therapies

A government initiative to provide psychological therapy on the NHS for people in England with a range of common mental health difficulties.

interpersonalpsychotherapy.org

International Society for Interpersonal Psychotherapy

Information about IPT and links to British organisations.

www.mind.org.uk

MIND

Charitable organisation offering information and support on mental health issues.

www.moodgym.anu.edu.au

MoodGYM

Interactive website using cognitive-behavioural techniques for people with depression and anxiety problems.

www.overcoming.co.uk

The 'Overcoming' series

A comprehensive array of books and self-help resources using cognitive-behavioural techniques to address a range of psychological difficulties, from alcoholism to weight problems.

www.rethink.org

Rethink

A national charity for everyone affected by mental illness.

Chapter 10

Lyubomirsky, S. (2010) *The How of Happiness: A Practical Guide to Getting the Life You Want*. Piatkus.

Nettle, D. (2006) *Happiness: The Science Behind Your Smile*. Oxford University Press.

Seligman, M. (2003) *Authentic Happiness: Using the New Positive Psychology to Realise Your Potential for Lasting Fulfilment*. Nicholas Brealey Publishing.

General

Brooks, D. (2012) *The Social Animal: The Story of How Success Happens*. Short Books.

www.bps.org.uk

The British Psychological Society

The website of the professional body that represents psychologists, which includes information on psychology as a career.

bps-research-digest.blogspot.co.uk

The British Psychological Society Research Digest

Up-to-date, easy-to-understand reports on the latest psychology findings, by Christian Jarrett.

www.spring.org.uk

Psyblog

Excellent, lively, easy-to-understand blog written by Jeremy Dean.

Key references

The latest editions of works are cited where possible.

Ainsworth, M. D. S., Blehar, M. C., Walters, E. and Wall, S. (1978) *Patterns of Attachment: A Psychological Study of the Strange Situation.* Erlbaum.

Allport, G. W. (1961) *Pattern and Growth in Personality.* Holt, Rinehart and Winston.

Asch, S. (1955) 'Opinion and social pressure', *Scientific American*, 193(5): 31–35.

Babiak, P. and Hare, R. D. (2007) *Snakes in Suits: When Psychopaths Go to Work.* Harper Collins.

Bandura, A., Ross, D and Ross, S. A (1961) 'Transmission of aggression through imitation of aggressive models', *Journal of Abnormal and Social Psychology*, 63(3): 575–82.

Baron-Cohen, S. (2012) *The Essential Difference: Men, Women and the Extreme Male Brain.* Penguin.

Baron-Cohen, S. (2012) *Zero Degrees of Empathy: A New Understanding of Human Cruelty and Kindness.* Penguin.

Bartholomew, K. and Horowitz, L. M. (1991) 'Attachment styles among young adults: a test of the four-category model', *Journal of Personality and Social Psychology*, 61(2): 226–44.

Bartlett, F. C. (1932) *Remembering: A Study in Experimental and Social Psychology.* Cambridge University Press.

Baumeister, R. F. (1997) *Evil: Inside Human Violence and Cruelty.* Holt.

Baumrind, D. (1978) 'Parental disciplinary patterns and social competence in children', *Youth and Society*, 9, 239–76.

Beck, A. T. (1991) *Cognitive Therapy and the Emotional Disorders.* Penguin.

Bowlby, J. (1951) *Maternal Care and Mental Health.* World Health Organization.

Christakis, N. A. and Fowler, J. H. (2009) *Connected: The Surprising Power of our Social Networks and How they Shape Our Lives.* Little, Brown and Co.

Clark, D. A. and Beck, A. T. (2011) *Cognitive Therapy of Anxiety Disorders: Science and Practice.* Guilford Press.

Cosmides, L. and Tooby, J. (1996) 'Cognitive adaptations for social exchange'. In *The Adapted Mind: Evolutionary Psychology and the Generation of Culture.* Oxford University Press.

Cosmides, L. and Tooby, J. (1997) *Evolutionary Psychology: A Primer.* Center for Evolutionary Psychology.

Damasio, A. (2006) *Descartes' Error: Emotion, Reason and the Human Brain.* Vintage.

Dunbar, R. (2011) *How Many Friends Does One Person Need? Dunbar's Number and Other Evolutionary Quirks.* Faber and Faber.

Ehrenreich, B. (2010) *Smile or Die: How Positive Thinking Fooled America and the World.* Granta Books.

Ekman, P. (2004) *Emotions Revealed.* Phoenix.

Ekman, P. (2009) *Telling Lies: Clues to Deceit in the Marketplace, Politics and Marriage.* W.W. Norton and Co.

Etcoff, N. (2000) *Survival of the Prettiest: The Science of Beauty.* Anchor Books.

Fine, C. (2011) *Delusions of Gender: The Real Science Behind the Sex Difference.* Icon Books Ltd.

Fisher, H. (2005) *Why We Love: The Nature and Chemistry of Romantic Love*. Holt McDougal.

Frankl, V. E. (2006) *Man's Search for Meaning*. Beacon Press.

Fredrickson, B. (2011) *Positivity: Groundbreaking Research to Release Your Inner Optimist and Thrive*. One World Publications.

Gerhardt, S. (2004) *Why Love Matters: How Affection Shapes a Baby's Brain*. Routledge.

Gilbert, D. (2007) *Stumbling on Happiness*. Harper Perennial.

Gilbert, P. (2010) *The Compassionate Mind*. Constable.

Goleman, D. (2007) *Social Intelligence: The New Science of Human Relationships*. Arrow.

Goleman, D. (2009) *Emotional Intelligence: Why It Can Matter More than IQ*. Bloomsbury.

The Gottman Relationship Institute (2012) www.gottman.com/49853/Research-FAQs.html (retrieved November 2012)

Haidt, J. (2012) *The Righteous Mind: Why Good People are Divided by Politics and Religion*. Pantheon.

Harlow, H.F. and Harlow, M. K. (1969) 'Effects of various mother-infant relationships on rhesus monkey behaviour'. In B. M. Foss (ed.) *Determinants of Infant Behaviour*. Methuen.

Hare, R. D. (1999) *Without Conscience: The Disturbing World of the Psychopaths Among Us*. Guilford Press.

Harris, J. R. (1999) *The Nurture Assumption*. Bloomsbury.

James, W. (1957) *The Principles of Psychology*. Dover Publications.

Jamison, K. R. (1996) *Touched with Fire: Manic-depressive Illness and the Artistic Temperament*. Simon and Schuster.

Kabat-Zinn, J. (2006) 'Mindfulness for Beginners'. Sounds True Inc.

Kahneman, D. (2011) *Thinking, Fast and Slow*. Penguin.

Loftus, E. F. and Palmer, J. C. (1974) 'Reconstruction of automobile destruction: An example of the interaction between language and memory', *Journal of Verbal Learning and Verbal Behaviour*, 13: 585–89.

Loftus, E. F. and Pickrell, J. E. (1995) 'The formation of false memories', *Psychiatric Annals*, 25: 720–25.

Lyubomirsky, S. (2010) *The How of Happiness: A Practical Guide to Getting the Life You Want*. Piatkus.

Maslow, A. (2011) *Toward a Psychology of Being*. Wilder Publications Ltd.

Milgram, S. (1974) *Obedience to Authority: An Experimental View*. Harper and Row.

Miller, G. (1956) 'The magical number seven plus or minus two: some limits on our capacity for processing information', *Psychological Review*, 63: 81–97.

Miller, G. (2001) *The Mating Mind: How Sexual Choice Shaped the Evolution of Human Nature*. Vintage.

Mischel, W., Ebbesen, E., Zeiss, A. (1972) 'Cognitive and attentional mechanisms in delay of gratification', *Journal of Personality and Social Psychology*, 21(2): 204–18.

Neisser, U. (1967) *Cognitive Psychology*. Prentice Hall.

Nettle, D. (2009) *Personality: What Makes You the Way You Are*. Oxford University Press.

Ofman, Daniel (2002) *Core Qualities: A Gateway to Human Resources*. Scriptum Publishers.

Pennebaker, J. W. (1997) 'Writing about emotional experiences as a therapeutic process', *Psychological Science*, 8(3): 162–66.

Piaget, J. and Inhelder, B. (1972) *The Psychology of the Child*. Basic Books.

Pinker, S. (1995) *The Language Instinct*. Penguin.

Pinker, S. (1999) *How the Mind Works.* Penguin.

Reiss, S. (2002) *Who Am I? The 16 Basic Desires that Motivate Our Actions and Define Our Personality.* Jeremy P Tarcher.

Salovey, P. and Mayer, J. D. (1990) 'Emotional Intelligence', *Imagination, Cognition and Personality,* 9: 185–211.

Seligman, M. (2012) *Flourish: A Visionary New Understanding of Happiness and Well-being.* Free Press.

Sherif, M., Harvey, O., White, B. J., Hood, W. and Sherif, C. (1961) 'Intergroup Conflict and Cooperation: The Robbers Cave Experiment'. Norman: University of Oklahoma, Insitute of Group Behaviour.

Skinner, B. F. (2002) *Beyond Freedom and Dignity.* Hackett Publishing Co.

Sternberg, R. and Sternberg, K. (2008) *The Nature of Hate.* Cambridge University Press.

Thaler, R. H. and Sunstein, C. R. (2009) *Nudge: Improving Decisions about Health, Wealth and Happiness.* Penguin.

Thompson-Cannino, C. J., Cotton, R. and Torneo, E. (2010) *Picking Cotton: Our Memoir of Injustice and Redemption.* St Martin's Griffin.

Thorndike, E. (1920) 'Intelligence and its uses', *Harper's Magazine,* 140, 227–35.

Tiedens, L. Z. (2001). 'Anger and advancement versus sadness and subjugation: The effects of negative emotion expressions on social status conferral', *Journal of Personality and Social Psychology,* 80, 86-94.

Watson, J. B., and Rayner, R. (1920) 'Conditioned emotional reactions', *Journal of Experimental Psychology,* 3, 1–14.

Zimbardo, P. (2008) *The Lucifer Effect: How Good People Turn Evil.* Rider.

Index